The Glorious Church

The Glorious Church
The Second Body of Christ

Dr. Fred Campbell

Townsend Press
Nashville, Tennessee

Copyright © 2022 by Dr. Fred Campbell

All right reserved. Printed in the United States of America.

Scripture quotations marked NIV are taken from the Holy Bible, New International Version. Copyright © 1973, 1978, 1984, 2011 by Biblica, Inc.® Used by permission. All rights reserved worldwide.

Scripture quotations marked NKJV are taken from the New King James Version. Copyright © 1982 by Thomas Nelson, Inc. Used by permission. All rights reserved.

Scripture quotations marked NASB are taken from the New American Standard Bible. Copyright © 1960, 1962, 1963, 1968, 1971, 1972, 1973, 1975, 1977, 1995 by The Lockman Foundation. Used by permission.

Scripture quotations marked ESV are taken from the Holy Bible, English Standard Version® (ESV®), Copyright© 2001 by Crossway, a publishing ministry of Good News Publishers. Used by permission. All rights reserved.

ISBN: 978-1-949052-94-7

*To my beloved sister,
Ms. Lula Mae Campbell,
with loving memories and appreciat*

Table Of Contents

PREFACE ix

ACKNOWLEDGMENTS xi

THE BEGINNING 1

CHAPTER 1
    The Bought 5

CHAPTER 2
    The Birthed 15

CHAPTER 3
    The Baptized 21

CHAPTER 4
    The Body 26

CHAPTER 5
    The Business 62

CHAPTER 6
    The Blessed 86

CHAPTER 7
    The Building 104

CHAPTER 8
    The Bride 110

CHAPTER 9
    The Bishop 121

CHAPTER 10
    The Breath 135

THE BIOGRAPHY: THE AUTHOR'S JOURNEY 149

THE EPILOGUE

    THE BONUS 155

        The Church in Defiance 156

        The Church in Deep Sleep 159

        The Church in Deception 163

        The Church in Decline 166

        The Church Delivered 168

A GLORIOUS CHURCH 172

NOTES 173

REFERENCES 176

ABOUT THE AUTHOR 178

Preface

Years ago, I was invited by Dr. Gwendolyn Prater to participate in a symposium sponsored by the School of Social Work on the campus of Jackson State University. The late Dr. Joseph Harrison Jackson was the keynote speaker for the event, and I distinctly remember the theme for that occasion being "What Can the Church Do to Help the Community?" The program was quite lengthy, and Dr. Jackson was not slated to speak until later in the evening. As a young pastor, I eagerly awaited with bated breath to hear from this sage. As I was on the edge of my seat, with my notepad and pen in hand, finally Dr. Jackson approached the podium rather slowly. He removed his glasses, as if to survey the audience, and then placed them back onto his face to read the theme aloud: "What Can the Church Do to Help the Community?" Assertively, he responded, "Let the church be the church," and then he went to his seat. I was astonished. I was shocked. And to say the least, I was perplexed because I was postured to take copious notes from this sagacious sage from the National Baptist Convention, USA, Incorporated. That night, I went home thoroughly disappointed.

Much later, I had an epiphany, an insightful revelation. Dr. Jackson's words were not simply a play on the theme, but rather they were a profound assertion that had eluded me. What Dr. Jackson simply stated was that what the community needed the most was for the church to be what God had called her to be. My personal interpretation is the reality that the church does the community the most good when the church is least like the community.

My friend and colleague Dr. Fred Campbell, in his book *The Glorious Church: The Second Body of Christ*, conveys exactly the very point that Dr. Jackson asserted nearly forty years ago at Jackson State University. What the world needs now, more than anything else, is an authentic,

New Testament church that understands its calling and purpose to be the salt and light of the whole world. To use Campbell's terminology, "We cannot be perceived nor referred to as the churchless community."

This book has rekindled for me my seminarian days. *The Glorious Church* offers a fresh perspective on the doctrine of the church for both the scholar and the student, as well as for the pastor and the parishioner. Campbell presents a systematic, theological approach on the church, both visible and invisible. He craftily superimposes concepts of the church (visible and invisible) in order to emphasize models of Christ's kingdom on earth as it is in heaven. Campbell's ten themes interweave his premise in such a manner that both a layperson and a scholar can benefit from the challenge to respond to Christ's clarion call to the church. His analogies of the church direct our local assemblies in both precept and practice in order to witness and work on behalf of the resurrected Christ, our Lord and Savior.

I congratulate my friend and my colleague for his distinct approach to teaching about Christ's visible church. This is a necessary body of work, a timely call to the modern church to be the church in this postmodern age. "Let the church be the church."

Dr. Jerry Young,
Pastor of the New Hope Baptist Church of Jackson, Mississippi
President of the National Baptist Convention, USA, Inc.

Acknowledgments

I am extremely grateful to the Mt. Zion Baptist Church for allowing me the freedom to author this book, *The Glorious Church*. My experience as shepherd and overseer of this fine congregation has been invaluable in the writing of this work.

Again, I am indebted to my editor, Mrs. Alicia Harris, who, without a doubt, is a gift to the body of Christ. I would also like to thank Pastor Maurice Harris, Alicia's husband, for allowing her to assist me in this project.

The Coronavirus pandemic and my health challenges enabled me to write this book while practicing social distancing and convalescing from my physical condition.

In writing this book my faith was tested, and I grew in faith. I learned much about me, and my love for Christ and His church deepened in the completion of this book. Praise God!

"All things do work together for them who love the Lord and are called according to His purpose."—Romans 8:28

The Beginning

Born not in aristocracy but born in obscurity and raised on the other side of the tracks in Nazareth, the carpenter's son and leader of a motley crew of men who became His disciples—this is the foundation of Christ's glorious church. When God established a nation, He called Abraham from the land of Ur of the Chaldeans; but when He established His church, He sent His Son through the Virgin Mary into the world, through the cross and empty tomb to Pentecost, thus birthing the church into His world.

To establish His church in the world, God went through great pain—from humanity to humiliation God came to establish His church. The incarnate God became the crucified God in order to create the church, people for His own possessions (1 Peter 2:9). Yes, to establish a nation He called a man; but to establish the church, God became man. While the nation Israel was the womb which God used to usher Himself into the world, He was creating something new—the extension of His incarnate presence, the glorious church. When we think "church" we must think of it as Christ's glorious presence of which we are members.

We trifle and toy with the local congregation of the church of Jesus Christ because we don't understand our stewardship of the holy. This cavalier response in the church may be due to the fact that within the local congregation are the wheat, the wicked, and the weak that cause the gloriousness to be distracted. There are imperfections in the assembly of God. Each member of the local congregation, who are members of the body of Christ, bring some form of imperfection. We must be aware that the local congregation is not yet the church triumphant. We are the church militant. There is fighting within and without. The church of Jesus Christ has the full attention of the devil, the flesh, and the world's sinful systems. Listen to the apostle Paul's warning to the Ephesian congregation:

> *"Pay careful attention to yourselves and to all the flock, in which the Holy Spirit has made you overseers, to care for the church of God, which he obtained with his own blood. I know that after my departure fierce wolves will come in among you, not sparing the flock; and from among your own selves will arise men speaking twisted things, to draw away the disciples after them. Therefore, be alert, remembering that for three years I did not cease night or day to admonish everyone with tears. And now I commend you to God and to the word of his grace, which is able to build you up and to give you the inheritance among all those who are sanctified"* (Acts 20:28-32, ESV).

We also notice the imperfections that can occur in congregations in Paul's instruction in Ephesians 4:17-32. He first spoke of the conduct of the unbeliever in verses 17-19, and contrasted the believer's conduct from the unbeliever's conduct in verses 20-23. But Paul admonishes the believers who are members of the Ephesian congregation to participate in the sanctification process in verses 24-32, reaching for righteousness and holiness. There is evidence here of imperfections, giving space for the devil through lying, anger, corrupt words, bitterness, clamor, evil speaking, wrath, malice and other forms of mistreatment. Kindness, tenderheartedness and forgiveness needed to be exercised within the congregation. Therefore, the church must also be penitent. It must become a grace place. Discipline is often necessary but grace-driven (see 1 Corinthians 5:1-12; 2 Corinthians 2:3-11). Yes! In the healing place, you and I can get hurt. The enemies of the church (the devil, the flesh and the world's system) will see to it. We should not be surprised of unchristian conduct in the church, but we should be surprised of ungrace in the church.

Grace should make us a nurturing and forgiving congregation, for we all are grace cases. Because of grace, the church ought to be a safe place to fail. It ought to be a safe place to become who we are in Christ Jesus (Philippians 3:12-16). The perfect church filled with perfect members is not of any use to God, who did not come for those who were well; rather, He sought those who were sick. The world of hopelessness needs evidence of hope that is found in those who are growing in grace knowledge. They need testimonies of the overcomers. They need those who are sick getting better because of mercy and grace. Yes! In the church militant there is the imperfect. There are imperfections in marriages, families, professions, schools, colleges, seminaries, fraternities, sororities, sport teams, businesses and clubs, and we don't leave those relationships or organizations, but we will leave and disassociate ourselves from the imperfect church. This, perhaps, tells us from the negative the significance of the church.

There are those who desire a churchless Christianity. There is the belief of some that they can encounter God apart from going to the church building. They feel that the majestic nature can bring them into the presence of God. They are averse not only to the building but also to so-called organized religion. Some of these people are "de-churched" persons who once attended casually or faithfully but were turned off for some reason. Is it possible to be "an unchurched Christian?" We will address the answer to this question later. When we do not understand the nature of the "glorious church" and the process, privilege, and purpose of belonging to her, we will speak in terms of a churchless Christianity.

The decline in church attendance will cause us to be intimidated by *"the few"* and in search of *"the many"* at any cost. Jesus had problems keeping *"the many"* (Matthew 7:13-14; John 6:60-71). Sunday worship is not necessarily for the unchurched. They are, at best, spectators to the Christian's *robust romance with the Redeemer*. The unchurched cannot worship God *"in spirit and in truth"* if the human spirit has not been quickened (John 4:24; Ephesians 2:1-5). To invite the unchurched and unsaved to join us in worship is in order. They may enjoy the experience without engaging in true worship, but they may encounter God in Christ while there. Much depends on how inviting is the life of the one who invites them to attend worship with them. Therefore, I do not believe that we are to design worship with sinners in mind, but for saints worshipping God. Although the worshipper must be hospitable to the unchurched and the unsaved, our purpose for gathering is to *"worship God"* (Revelation 19:10), not to placate sinners. While we want sinners to be comfortable, we also want them to be uncomfortable in their lostness (Acts 2:37-41).

I believe the post-Christian era is upon us. There is the falling away from the faith from within the fellowship (1 Timothy 4:1-5), and there is rejection of faith outside the fellowship of the unbeliever (Romans 1:18-32). The United States of America is no longer known in name as *"A Christian Nation."* It is more paganistic in its religious construct. Postmodernism of uncertainty is certain that there is no objective truth. This *"ism"* leaves room for the idolatry of humanism, which is its own religion.

In the midst of these times, the glorious church is indestructible. Although, the glorious glow is often dimmed by our inauthentic witness in the world, we must not fret when seeing the falling away and the rejection of Christ and His church. In this book, I hope to explain why we should be encouraged in these discouraging times.

Chapter 1

The Bought

"It wasn't deeded to Him; He bled to obtain it."

"Pay careful attention to yourselves and to all the flock, in which the Holy Spirit has made you overseers, to care for the church of God, which he obtained with his own blood."—Acts 20:28, ESV

The glorious church exists because Jesus Christ paid for it with His blood. He redeemed the church by offering His life as ransom for many in order to become one glorious church. Jesus became our kinsman redeemer to create His second body on earth. Much is suggested in this matter of redemption. Why did He need to redeem us? Why was it necessary that He buy us back? It suggests that we once were His and we went rogue; we went astray from the owner.

Here is the essence of sin—humanity going astray from Divinity. It is living a life independent from the "I Am" God. Sin is contextualized in the notion of humanism. It is man come of age in God's house. It is the steward acting like owner. Sin is the human disposition egocentrism. The prophet described sin in this way:

"All we like sheep have gone astray; We have turned, every one, to his own way; And the LORD has laid on Him the iniquity of us all" (Isaiah 53:6, NKJV).

Sin is the slave desiring freedom from the Master. The fact of God as creator makes Him owner of His creation:

"The earth is the Lord's, and all its fullness, The world and those who dwell therein" (Psalm 24:1, NKJV).

Man is steward of all "therein" the world, including himself. He was created for God. Man finds being and purpose in God. As a fish's existence is found in water and the plant finds its existence in the soil, so man finds his existence in God. Thus, fish and plant will eventually die outside their existential context. Apart from relationship with God, mankind is spiritually dead and will be eternally separated from God.

Redemption is about the return of the slave to his master. I know this slave language is insensitive to those who have or may be experiencing social injustice and systemic racism, but it is the language of Scripture in describing our relationship either with God or with Satan. Let me quote some of these passages:

> *"What then? Shall we sin because we are not under law but under grace? Certainly not! Do you not know that to whom you present yourselves slaves to obey, you are that one's slaves whom you obey, whether of sin leading to death, or of obedience leading to righteousness? But God be thanked that though you were slaves of sin, yet you obeyed from the heart that form of doctrine to which you were delivered. And having been set free from sin, you become slaves of righteousness"* (Romans 6:15-18, NKJV).

> *"For perhaps he departed for a while for this purpose, that you might receive him forever, no longer as a slave but more than a slave—a beloved brother, especially to me but how much more to you, both in the flesh and in the Lord"* (Philemon 1:15-16, NKJV).

In the Old Testament book of Hosea, there is an historical illustration of redemption lived out in the life of the prophet who was told to redeem his wife from a life of whoredom. This prophet's marriage illustrated the spiritual condition of Israel. As the prophet was to redeem his wife, so God was prepared to redeem Israel from their whoredom. In marriage, Hosea's wife, Gomer, belonged to him but went astray with others. Please! Listen to these redemptive words:

> *Then the* LORD *said to me, "Go again, love a woman who is loved by lover and is committing adultery, just like the love of the* LORD *for the children of Israel, who look to other gods and love the raisin cakes of the pagans." So, I bought her for myself for fifteen shekels of silver, and one and one of silver, and one and one-half homers of barley. And I said to her, "you shall stay with me many days; you shall not play the harlot, nor shall you have a man—so, too, will I be toward you"* (Hosea 3:1-3, NKJV).

Hosea paid a slave's redemption cost for who was once his, which is what Jesus Christ did. In human redemption, Jesus paid with His life for those who rightly belonged to Him prior to going astray. Like Hosea, Jesus came after humanity. He made the first move. He initiated the redemptive process—that is, God did, in the fall of our primal parents when He came anthropomorphically walking, looking to redeem Adam and Eve, and provided redemptive covering for their nakedness (Genesis 3:6-21).

In Acts 20:28, we are told that the church belongs to God. It is the church of God. If the earth is the Lord's and everything in it is His, why does He need to purchase it? Isn't it automatically His? Is it because man sold himself to sin, an instrument to unrighteousness? Does He pay ransom to Satan? Certainly not! Does He purchase or obtain the church for Himself and not from anyone? Is this simply but profoundly obtaining freedom from sin's slavery for those who make up the church? This one verse is packed with theological questions. Whose blood purchased or obtained the church? It looks like it was God's blood, but we know it was His Son's blood, who became flesh in order to bleed out His life for the church. Because of the hypostatic union of the two natures of Jesus Christ, the writer Luke was inspired to infer that God purchased the church with His own blood. Jürgen Moltmann titled one of his theological works *The Crucified God* because he understood that, in the Trinity, when one works it is in harmony with the other persons in the Godhead. This unity was not viewed by Moltmann as tritheism—three separate gods, or modalism, which is the belief that God plays different roles; but although there is unity, there are distinct persons in the Trinity. Did God die? No, God did not die, but the Son of God, who became man, died as real men do. The one nature of the hypostatic union died.

Through this redemptive act of purchasing the church, comprehensive oneness is created. The sinner, through the atonement, is made at-one with God, vertically, and at-one with one another horizontally. In salvation, there is the new man who fits into the Holy Communion of the church. We will study this more in the following chapters. However, through Jesus' blood, the church was brought into being. It never existed before. Therefore, Jesus did not purchase it from anyone, rather He created it for Himself. He acquired and obtained it for Himself. The idea of belonging must be understood. It is His church. He built something brand new. He owns the church. Therefore, it is not Israel reshaped into the church, although the church commenced with Jewish members. The church is Christ's creation strictly for Himself for the sake of the world. This called-out assembly was gushed out into the world by Jesus' blood. Thus, "*brought* the church" might be better than "*bought* the church." The King James Version of the Bible offers the word *purchased,* while it might be more accurate to say "obtained or acquired" the church."

Christ's ownership includes both the invisible and the visible church. The holy catholic, universal church is comprised of the local congregation which is a microcosm of the body of Christ. He cannot disown the church even in its imperfections. But through *"sanctification He is constantly cleansing her by the washing of the word in order to present her to Himself in splendor, without spot or wrinkle or any such thing, that she might be holy and without blemish"* (Ephesians 5:26-27—personal emphasis). Yes! The militant church and the triumphant belongs to Him. The gloriousness of the church is seen in its grandeur, greatness and grace, as a church and people there are treasure in trash (2 Corinthians 4:7). Yes, He owns us in our weaknesses, probably more than in our strengths (2 Corinthians 12:1-10).

Knowing that Christ Jesus bought the church means He is owner and head of His church. The church is His, not ours. His lordship and ownership are implied in the fact that He has acquired the church by way of His blood. Both pastor and people must get it into our heads, the church belongs to Him and Him alone. At best we are stewards and caretakers of His body, the church, and we need the Holy Spirit to manage His purpose for His church on earth. Since the church is one body with many members, each individual member has been bought, making the whole body bought with the same purchase price of His blood. We are under new ownership. The apostle Paul challenges the saints in Corinth that their total selves belong to God when he wrote:

> *"Flee from sexual immorality. Every other sin a person commits is outside the body, but the sexually immoral person sins against his own body. Or do you not know that your body is a temple of the Holy Spirit within you, whom you have from God? You are not your own, for you were bought with a price. So, glorify God in your body"* (1 Corinthians 6:18-20, ESV).

We, like the Corinthians, are called to glorify God in our physical bodies because they belong to God; for they were created, and we were re-created to glorify God in that body for the sake of Christ's body. Our physical bodies are His, and the church, which is the body of Christ, is

His, and both exist for His glory. He has purchased the church for His glorious purpose, and those who belong to the church belong to Him.

> *"Do you not know that you are God's temple and that God's Spirit dwells in you? If anyone destroys God's temple, God will destroy him. For God's temple is holy, and you are that temple"*
> (1 Corinthians 3:16-17, ESV).

The Scripture verse above speaks of the church as God's temple. The Spirit of God indwells each member of the church and the church itself. The Spirit's presence in the believer indicates ownership (see 2 Corinthians 1:22; Ephesians 1:13-14). But this ownership is somewhat paradoxical in nature. It is a negative-positive in the redemptive process. The believers in the body of Christ are both slaves and sons. In redemption, sinners are set free from the wrath of God to enter the family of God. We are freed from the slavery of sin and unrighteousness to the slavery of obedient righteousness (Romans 6:15-23). In redemption, God repurchases us for Himself in order for us to return to our boughtness—purposed humanity—lost in the first Adam and gained again in the Second Adam's redemptive act (Genesis 1:27; Romans 3:23; 2 Corinthians 5:17). Jesus makes possible all of this through His atonement. He who is one with God in Trinity and became one with man in humanity was exclusively able to mediate between the holy and the unholy (1 Timothy 2:5-6).

This "boughtness" must not be viewed in the same light of the heinous subjugation of human beings in American slavery. Rather, we must think of this "boughtness" as that of Jacob's love for Rachel that drove him to serve fourteen years to gain her for his wife. His service to Laban was an act of purchasing (Genesis 29:1-29). God paid the price for us with the giving of His Son. He so loved, therefore He so gave—not fourteen years, but His Son, who gave His life to buy our pardon (John 3:16). Jesus Christ bought the church and its members to be His beloved bride for His purpose and pleasure. The redemptive price was the price of our adoption into God's family (Romans 8:12-17). To be a slave son and daughter in the family/church of God is a glorious reality when we think about how we were once slaves of sin and subjects of Satan walking against the righteousness of God. To be a slave of Christ, bought by His precious blood, should be an honor of grace.

Called-out is the term we often use when identifying the church. It is a secular designation for a classical Greek assembly as we see in Acts 19:39-41. The Greek word, *ekklesia*, means the called-out assembly. However, later the Greek word *kyriakon* distinguishes the assembly in a more preferable way as "the Lord's house" (1 Corinthians 11:20). This definition relates to Jesus' declaration that "upon this rock I will build my church" (Matthew 16:18). It is the Lord's church. Lordship salvation is objected by some because it appears to be a form of works. And salvation is a matter of grace alone through faith alone. To insist on lordship salvation is to rule out grace through faith alone. Some seem to suggest that Christ being our Lord is optional. We are simply saved by believing in Jesus Christ as our Savior. They further believe that Jesus becomes Lord in the process of sanctification. As the Christian grows, Christ becomes Lord, and the maturing Christian declares that He is Lord. May I say at this point of contention that one cannot save that which He does not possess. You have to own it before you can save it. It has been said, "Christ is either Lord of all or He is not Lord at all." Jesus is Lord. We cannot make Him Lord. Our declaration that He is Lord is a mere acknowledgement, though, not placing Him on the throne of our lives. If He is Savior, He is also at the same time Lord. In salvation, when we surrendered to who Jesus Christ is and what He has done through the cross and resurrection, it was surrendering to His saviorhood and lordship at the same time. If Jesus bought you and me through His blood, we are His and He owns us. We are His possession, and we are now under new management. He is

Owner, Ruler, Master, and Lord. We have been bought with the precious blood of Jesus and we are no longer our own (1 Corinthian 6:19-20). Everyone who is in the Lord's house is under the lordship of Christ.

I see nowhere in Scripture where Jesus as Lord is an afterthought in salvation. I do not see lordship as something extra in salvation or mature status of obedience in salvation. It is part and parcel to salvation (Acts 2:21; 2:36; 16:31; Romans 10:9-10). The crucified life (Galatians 2:20) renders Christ as Lord. To be a slave of God renders God as Master (Romans 6:22; Ephesians 6:5-7). The life of the resurrected cannot be other than under the new dominion (Romans 6:9, 14). Jesus is Lord of His church and her members. We must note that in the New Testament Jesus is known by Lord more than Savior.

Boughtness and belongingness is associated with the idea of the kingdom of God/heaven. Jesus as King, Lord, and Master has a kingdom. It is not of this world (John 18:36) but is commensurate in His coming, is in continuum in those who have bowed to the king and will be consummated in the age to come. It is in the world but not of the world. The kingdom is paradoxical, in that, it is a present reality, meaning that it is here but yet it is coming in the future. The church is the colony of the kingdom. It is not the kingdom but as ambassadors the church represents the kingdom in the kingdom of darkness (Colossians 1:13). Yes! The kingdom has come, **and** it is coming. Jesus taught the disciple to pray: "Your kingdom come, your will be done, on earth as it is in heaven" (Matthew 6:10, ESV). Lloyd Ogilvie in his book, *The Autobiography of God*, states, "Before you can be in the kingdom, the kingdom must first be in you."[1] Jesus told Nicodemus that he could not see nor enter the kingdom of God unless he was born again (John 3:1-8). As we are birthed into the kingdom, so are we birthed into the church, the colony of the kingdom.

The glorious church is Christ's precious possession. He gave His life that it might exist in the world for His glory. It is a glorious church because Christ is present on earth through His church.

A vivid description of the cost of our membership in the body of Christ is prophetically rendered in Isaiah 53. The old preacher poetically said that Isaiah stood on the mountain of prophetical splendor and looked down the corridors of time and said that Jesus was "wounded for our transgressions, He was bruised for our iniquities; the chastisement for our peace was upon Him, and by His stripes we are healed" (Isaiah 53:5, ESV). Martin Luther called John 3:16 "the Gospel in Miniature." I believe Isaiah's prophetic description of the Suffering Servant answers the question of how much did *"God so love[d] the world?"* (John 3:16, NKJV). Isaiah's query: *"Who has believed our report/preaching"* presupposes rejection of the messenger and the message, leading to suffering and death. Although, the sufferings were caused by those whom Jesus came to save, His sufferings were good news. The actions of wicked men worked out for our good, for they played a role in God's redemptive plan. They were guilty in their hearts of persecuting him to death, but all sinners are guilty of His death. However, Jesus was there on the cross because God purposed and produced this ugly drama, the Son directed it and was the starring Actor, and the Holy Spirit choreographed it. Isaiah said, *"It pleased the Lord to bruise Him"* (Isaiah 53:10, NKJV). The miracle in the death of Jesus was that He was in control of His own death (John 10:18-20). He did die, but He had to orchestrate His own death. Jesus did not simply *have* life, He *was* life, and *is* life (John 14:6). Therefore, out of obedience, He surrendered to death (Philippians 2:8). Life is older than death, and it will outlast death (1 Corinthians 15:26). In fact, death died in Jesus' death (1 Corinthians 15:54-57). He conquered death not in the Resurrection, but in His death. Death has an expiration date on it (Revelation 21:4). Now let us turn our attention to Isaiah's description of the cost of our membership in the body of Christ.

Jesus grew up in obscurity, scandal, and in dry ground of Nazareth.

He had little appeal, thus He was despised and rejected by His countrymen. He was not desirable as a person, only as a miracle worker. His own family questioned His sanity (Mark 3:20-21). Jesus carried the burden of His ultimate purpose throughout His life. We notice in Gethsemane the weight of it all (Matthew 26:38-46). The sins of the whole world would be laid on Him (Isaiah 53:4-5).

Chapter 2

The Birthed

"It is not a matter of joining, but birthing."

"Jesus answered, 'Truly, truly, I say to you, unless one is born of water and the Spirit, he cannot enter the kingdom of God.'"—John 3:5, ESV

It was an eventful night. Nicodemus came to Jesus to enquire of Him for the miracles pointed him to Jesus' exceptionality. But Jesus interrupted his query with a strange truth that challenged his Jewishness and Hebraic pedigree. It was not an optional challenge rather an imperative. For the kingdom of God was not automatically his. Nicodemus needed to experience the new birth to realize and enter the kingdom. The natural birth made spiritual birth necessary. Neither Nicodemus' humanism nor his religiosity could usher him into the kingdom of God. He thought he was an insider when all the time he was outside. So many who are religious and moral think they are in the will and purpose of God when in actuality they are outsiders. This Pharisee, the so-called custodian of the Law, was far from the kingdom of God. He thought he was near, but he was far off. Now, Nicodemus was near the kingdom in the presence of Jesus, but yet far like the scribe in Mark 12:34. The people of promise are nearer, but in their rejection of Jesus they are pushed away (John 1:11-13), and the Gentiles who were far are now near by the blood of Jesus (Ephesians 2:13).

Jesus's encounter with Nicodemus helps us to understand that the church is not necessarily replacing Israel in salvation history. Israel has not become the church. Israel are the people of God through human birth and the church is the people of God through the new birth. Both are the product of faith, but being birthed into the church through faith is more dynamic.

The new birth, known theologically as regeneration, is the experience of each member of the body of Christ. It is an individual experience. Like Nicodemus, the believer must be born again. When grace reaches down and faith reaches up in helplessness, the dynamic of the new birth takes place wherein the old nature is transformed into the new nature. The caterpillar becomes the butterfly. The new birth is not an addition but a transformation of the old into the new. In the miracle of the new birth there is also the birthing into the new community known as *the church*. Through the physical birth we enter into the world, but through the spiritual birth we enter into the church. Listen again to these words of Jesus: *"And I also say to you that you are Peter, and on this Rock, I will build My church, and gates of hades shall not prevail against it"* (Matthew 16:18, NKJV). The new birth is the nature of Christ in the believer. The verse just quoted let us know that Jesus promised to build His church out of that which is applicable to His nature. Peter possessed Jesus' rocky nature. Jesus was *the* Rock and Peter was *a* rock. Jesus is saying "of Me I will build the church." In the "My" is the possessive pronoun of ownership, and also the implied "of Me" denotes the nature of the church. The membership will be comprised of those who have been born again. The universal church, not the local congregation, is comprised only of the born again. The local congregation may have a mixture of the unborn and the born again. What makes the body of Christ glorious is that it consists of those who have experienced the mysterious new birth. And it is that experience that ushers the believer into the universal church.

The requirement for membership in the church is regeneration. In regeneration the sinner is acted upon. Perhaps reformation works for membership in other institutions of men, but not so in the church of Jesus Christ. People can change into better and productive people. They can make changes without divine intervention. There may be behavior modifications through psychological means. Those bound by various addictions can experience freedom. There is also prison reform for criminals who have been rehabilitated through programs inside the penal institution. But the church requires regeneration, the change of the old nature into the new. It is the inward work of God.

> *"Blessed be the God and Father of our Lord Jesus Christ! According to his great mercy, he has caused us to be born again to a living hope through the resurrection of Jesus Christ from the dead, to an inheritance that is imperishable, undefiled, and unfading, kept in heaven for you, who by God's power are being guarded through faith for a salvation ready to be revealed in the last time"* (1 Peter 1:3-5, ESV).

> *"But as many as received Him, to them He gave the right to become children of God, to those who believe in His name: who were born, not of blood, nor of the will of the flesh, nor of the will of man, but of God"* (John 1:12-13, NKJV).

Regeneration is more than a behavioral change. The old nature that makes us behave in unrighteousness has been changed in order that we might behave in righteousness.

> *"Therefore, if anyone is in Christ, he is a new creation; old things have passed away; behold, all things have become new"* (2 Corinthians 5:17, NKJV).

> *"But God be thanked that though you were slaves of sin, yet you obeyed from the heart that form of doctrine to which you were delivered. And having been set free from sin, you became slaves of righteousness"* (Romans 6:17-18, NKJV).

The various metaphors illustrate this birthing. Members as living stones placed into the edifice as stated in Ephesians 2:19-22 and 1 Peter 2:4-8 illustrate this dynamic relation with Christ and His church. The church as the household of God along with the doctrine of adoption speak of family life, like a birthing into the family, the church. Adoption is related to regeneration and justification but different. It is a judicial act of grace. It is family-related but not life-lived in the believer as is true of regeneration. Yes! It is sonship, but in status. However, the generative act of grace is the new life, the new man, the new creation, the eternal life, the resurrection life, the abundant life, and the life hidden in Christ Jesus (Colossians 3:3; 1 John 5:11-12). Only those regenerated are adopted into the family of God and members of the body of Christ. Bearing the image of God does not make man a child of God (John 1:12-13). Man is but a creature of God and only in this sense is he the offspring of God (Acts 17:25-29). But only the new creature becomes children of God. Only the new creature has received the Spirit of adoption (Romans 8:15) making the Fatherhood of God exclusively that of the born again. God is only our (the believer's) Father (Matthew 6:9). He is the Father of those in the colony of the kingdom—the church of Jesus Christ. This adoption, working intrinsically with regeneration, through justification and sanctification (1 John 3:1-3) makes clear our sonship and God's Fatherhood as exclusive. He is our Father. What an intimate distinction! It is a nearness to the transcendent God wherein He is Daddy God and not dreadful God. Through our relationship with His Son, the second Person, we have access to the Father, the first Person, in the power of the Holy Spirit, the third Person (Ephesians 2:18).

Peter is a rock situated in Christ Jesus, the Rock and we also are living stones, structured by the Chief Cornerstone, to fit into the edifice of the church. Again, we speak of the miracle in this union with Christ. It is a spiritual reality and is as much a miracle as life itself.

"If then you have been raised with Christ, seek the things that are above, where Christ is, seated at the right hand of God. Set your minds on things that are above, not on things that are on earth. For you have died, and your life is hidden with Christ in God. When Christ who is your life appears, then you also will appear with Him in glory" (Colossians 3:1-4, ESV).

In our membership in the body of Christ we share His life. The Christian life is Christ's life lived in the believer. This is the new life in regeneration that makes possible the new position of adoption because of the new standing in justification.

The only way to enter the body of Christ is that you must be born again. You must have the life of Christ to enter the church, the colony of the kingdom of God on earth. It is a new kind of life. It is not an add on, the old is passed and the new has come (2 Corinthians 5:17). There is an ending and then a new beginning. The old cannot exist in the sphere of the new. Lazarus could not be dead and alive at the same time (John 11:43-44). The old man and the new man cannot exist at the same time but the residue of the old must constantly be removed. The grave clothes of Lazarus must through sanctification be replaced with practical righteousness (Romans 6:15-19). We must not keep going back to the grave of our past; but rather press on towards the mark and goal of our newness (Philippians 3:12-14; Romans 6:4).

There is no such thing as a churchless Christianity. Membership in the body of Christ, of which the local congregation is a microcosm, is not a matter of human choice. It is indicative of the new birth. While membership in the local congregation is a choice, membership in the universal church, the body of Christ is the result of a generative act of grace that ought to be appreciated by not forsaking assembling (Hebrews 10:25). At the birth of the church on the Day of Pentecost, the reality of membership in the body of Christ was manifested in the forming of the local church and churches on earth. Here at Pentecost, the invisible church became the visible church. Those Jews and, perhaps proselytes, were born again, saved, entered the body of Christ and were added to the numbers of the visible church, the local congregation (Acts 2:37-41). It has been said that "birds of a feather flock together!" Those of common faith who have experienced the Gospel of grace and regenerative grace will enter koinonia—fellowship with brothers and sisters, as we will see in the next chapter. Christian fellowship is important to the church's witness in the world. What a fellowship! It is more than social gathering and social greetings. It is the indispensable union of believers in connection with the Head of the church. It is mutual sharing of the life of Christ in community (1 John 1:6-7). We cannot have fellowship with God without having fellowship with one another. This calls for relating in the visible church.

Chapter 3

The Baptized

"It isn't merely personal, but interpersonal."

"In one Spirit we were all baptized into one body—Jews or Greeks, slaves or free—and all were made to drink of one Spirit."—1 Corinthians 12:13, ESV

The glorious church is the mysterious reality of Spirit baptism. There is Spirit birth, sharing the life of Christ (John 3:6), and then there is Spirit baptism where in the body of Christ we share life together. There is the vertical and then the horizontal miracle. In multifaceted salvation, there is the work of the Holy Spirit in regeneration; new life in justification; new standing in adoption; new position in sanctification; new character in Spirit baptism; and new relationships with Christ and other believers in the body of Christ.

The baptism of the Spirit is the reality of salvation. The indwelling and the baptism of the Spirit are not some second blessing of the Holy Spirit for super saints. Every believer has the gift of the Spirit (Acts 2:38, 39). Much has been made of the second blessing of the Spirit based on Acts 19:2. There were some of John the Baptist's disciples who had not come to Christ, they were stuck on John. Paul asked them, *"Did you receive the Holy Spirit when you believed."* The King James Version says *"since you believed."* It sounds like the Spirit is an afterthought and the experience of some. All believers experience this mysterious and miraculous phenomenon when grace reaches down, and faith reaches up in helplessness to God in Christ. The narrative of the Acts of the Apostles makes it seem like the indwelling and baptism come after initial salvation, but it does not follow salvation, it is part and partial to salvation. If you have been born of the Spirit, you also have been indwelled and baptized by the Spirit. No Spirit, no salvation **at all** (Romans 8:9). The indwelling declares belongingness. The baptism of the Spirit declares belonging to one another in the body of Christ.

The evidence of the baptism of the Spirit is seen in all the "one another" statements:

"A new commandment I give to you that you love one another; as I have loved you, that ye also love one another. By this all will know that you are My disciples, if you have love for one another" (John 13:34-35, NKJV).

"You brethren, have been called to liberty; only do not use liberty as an opportunity for the flesh, but through love serve one another" (Galatians 5:13, NKJV).

"Bearing with one another, and forgiving one another, if anyone has a complaint against another; even as Christ forgive you, so you also must do" (Colossians 3:13, NKJV).

"Brethren, if a man is overtaken in any trespass, you who are spiritual restore such a one in a spirit of gentleness, considering yourself lest you also be tempted. Bear one another's burdens, and so fulfill the law of Christ" (Galatians 6:1-2, NKJV).

"Be kind to one another, tenderhearted, forgiving one another, even as God in Christ forgave you" (Ephesians 4:32, NKJV).

The evidence of the baptism of the Spirit is functioning in interrelationship with one another in the body of Christ. It is doing life together. Yes! We are baptized into the one anotherness. True fellowship is realizing our one anotherness and embracing it like our spiritual lives depended on it (Ephesians 2:11-22). This fellowship is greatly enabled by the life we share in the body of Christ (2 Peter 1:4). There will be differences, but this must not deter our fellowship. As living stones, we must not seek uniformity and sameness, but diversity in unity. The blood of Jesus has created nearness in the body of Christ, not sameness. We will notice this in the gifting in the body of Christ (1 Corinthians 12:4-7). In this new man, the church of Jesus Christ is the source of our fellowship. The church is not a coalition, but a communion of the one anotherness. The church is the creation of a brand-new humanity, anchored in the second Adam, Jesus Christ. This fellowship is not a conglomeration, but rather one new man. It is the answer to Jesus' intercessory prayer:

> *"Holy Father, keep them in your name, which you have given me that they may be one, even as we are one"* (John 17:11, ESV).

The baptism of the Spirit is the means of this oneness. This plural oneness is the essence of the mystery of the Trinity and the nature of Christian marriage (Matthew 28:19-20; Ephesians 5:31). Monotheism is the central teaching of Judaism, Islam, and Christianity. However, Christianity audaciously departs from both Judaism and Islam in its Trinitarian doctrine. One God in three distinct persons. Oneness is still essential to the Christian faith, but plural oneness. The mystery of God is deepened in this Trinitarian doctrine. However, it gives definition to the nature of the church—one body with many members, and the nature of Christian marriage—the two becoming one flesh.

Let me note here that Jesus is not said to have baptized during His earthly ministry. However, He is the baptizer in His post-earthy ministry. The Holy Spirit is the agent, but Jesus is the baptizer.

> *"I indeed baptize you with water unto repentance: but he that cometh after me is mightier than I, whose shoes I am not worthy to bear he shall baptize you with the Holy Ghost, and with fire: Whose fan is in his hand, and he will thoroughly purge his floor, and gather his wheat into the garner; but he will burn up the chaff with unquenchable fire"* (Matthew 3:11-12, KJV).

There is the baptism of the believer into the new relationship that Jesus miraculously performs through the agency of the Holy Spirit, and there also is the baptism of the unbelievers into judgment. It is an immersion into the one anotherness, forming an indispensable union in the body of Christ. The one Spirit is the agent, forming the one body of diverse people, indwelt by the one Spirit. What a union! The Spirit in us and us in the Spirit (John 3:34). We have all of the Spirit while He might not have all of us. We are filled with oneness (Ephesians 4:4-7) and placed into oneness in the one body of Christ. We do not have the Spirit in measures (Romans 8:9). We do not have to say "Come, Holy Spirit." He indwells us completely while He does not have us completely (Ephesians 5:18). Therefore, there is no need for a so-called second working of the Spirit. Those early saints who waited on the advent of the Spirit were saved prior to the advent into them; however, it was no second working of the Spirit. It was the initial work of the Spirit in the life of the new church. So, His initial work was the baptism and the indwelling in the believer, forming the body of Christ and indwelling the church through its members.

Christians play with the church when they lose sight of the interpersonal reality of the body of Christ of which their local congregation is a member. Members abuse and harm one another when they lose sight of their oneness. This is not a new problem in the church for we hear it and observe it in the Corinthians church. We see it in the division, strife, and immorality inside the fellowship of the saints.

Chapter 4

The Body

"It is the incarnate becoming the reincarnate."

"As in one body we have many members, and the members do not all have the same function, so we, though many, are one body in Christ, and individually members one of another."—Romans 12:4-5, ESV

"Just as the body is one and has many members, and all the members of the body, though many, are one body, so it is with Christ."—1 Corinthians 12:12, ESV

A metaphor is not literally applicable. It is normally a figure of speech applied to an object or action. But the biblical use of the word *body* transcends the definition of a metaphor as a spiritual reality of the makeup of the church of Jesus Christ. The metaphor of the church as the household of God, the temple of God, and the family of God are different from understanding the church as the body of Christ. For the church is indeed an organism. It is the living body of Christ on earth. The church is an organized organism structured by the headship of Christ and by Christ, the Chief Cornerstone of the church with body functioning. This body is as real as the incarnated body of Christ, born of the Spirit (Matthew 1:18). The members who comprise the church are born of the Spirit (John 3:5-8). According to the Acts' narrative, the advent of the Spirit and the birth of the church are synonymous (Acts 1:1-11). The kingdom that they thought of was not the kingdom that Jesus spoke of. The promised Spirit would baptize them into the church, the colony of the kingdom of God. These men in particular were foundation members of the church—charter members (if you will)—of the church of Jesus Christ, and they would become His witnesses, in particular, but not exclusively. Jesus looked directly at them and said, *"You will be my witnesses."* It was a corporate look and not an individual look. Those baptized into the body of Christ, together, will be His witnesses. You shall become a witnessing community.

The purpose of the second body of Christ, the reincarnated body of Christ, is to be His witness in the world. The devil knew the death and resurrection of Jesus was just the beginning of His effectuality in the world (Acts 1:1) and more was to come (John 14:11-17) through His church empowered by the Spirit. The Incarnation is in continuum through the second body of Christ. I dare to call it the reincarnation of Christ. The Spirit of truth resides in each member of the body, in order to tell the truth about Jesus Christ who is the Truth (John 14:6; 16:13). C. Norman Kraus was on point when he said: "The church, not the individual, is the body of Christ in mission. Individuals are members of the body, and the gifts of the Spirit are entrusted to them as resources for the mission of the body."[2] The missional purpose of the church, the body of Christ, as the new man has become flesh, is communicating the truth about Jesus in the power of the Spirit of truth. Kraus further says, concerning the church as the witnessing community, that "the community does not proclaim itself, but is itself the witness."[3] And, "to be in Christ is to be in solidarity with Him through participation in His body. The new being is individual—in—authentic community."[4] Then Kraus, in reference to 1 Corinthians 11:20-22, 29, states that Paul "reminded them that as a whole group they were 'God's temple' (1 Corinthians 3:16). They shared a common Spirit by whom they were baptized into one body (1 Corinthians 12:13). They were, he told them, individually members of [the body of Christ] (1 Corinthians 12:27), and each individual's gift was for the common good.'"[5] Jürgen Moltmann in answering his own question, "Is the church the other Christ?"[6] answers by saying, "The church is the body of Christ. The body and the head together are Christ. Christ is therefore only Christ in the full sense together with the church."[7] The church is the body of Christ but not absent of Christ as Head. The body alone cannot be the Christ. Christ is still with us through His body, but not with a decapitated body (1 Corinthians 11:3; Ephesians 5:23; Colossians 1:18).

The glorious church has privilege and responsibility. As the body of Christ, we are the community of the restored glory. In Adam, we come short of the glory of God (Romans 3:23), but in Christ's body we become the community of the restored image. In the Incarnation, Jesus Christ is the image of the invisible God (Colossians 1:15-20). In the reincarnation, or the extended incarnation, we reveal the image of the Son (Romans 8:29). What a privilege! As the body of Christ, we glorify Him. Paul tells us that the church, as Christ's body, exists for the praise of His glory (Ephesians 1:11-14). This is both privilege and responsibility.

In the pre-Pentecost descriptions of the church as the body of Christ, we should understand that glorifying God is not only in our worship of praise, but our presence of behavior. We hear this in Jesus' discourse called the Sermon on the Mount.

"You are the salt of the earth, but if salt has lost its taste, how shall its saltiness be restored? It is no longer good for anything except to be thrown out and trampled under people's feet. You are the light of the world. A city set on a hill cannot be hidden. Nor do people light a lamp and put it under a basket, but on a stand, and it gives light to all in the house. In the same way, let your light shine before others, so that they may see your good works and give glory to your Father who is in heaven" (Matthew 5:13-16, ESV).

When Jesus spoke to His disciples on the mount, He was speaking to those who would be charter members of the body of Christ. The kingdom was certainly in view. However, it was the kingdom of the not yet living in the now. It was the preview of the church, the colony of the kingdom. The use of the emphatic pronouns "you are" announces exclusivity. You alone are the salt and light on earth and in the world. With specificity He speaks of those who would form the body of Christ as foundational leaders and members of the new community. The glorified church would be responsible for influencing righteousness above rightness and rottenness (Proverbs 14:12; Philippians 2:15). The church is the city on the hill, as distinct and different, but in the midst of darkness as children of light (1 Thessalonians 5:5; Ephesians 5:8). Both salt and light are ontological in their presence. The church is video and not mere audio. The church must become music and then lyrics. We are salt and light. The church is the communicative character of community and its members. While Jesus is the Light of the World, His church and its members are lights in the world. As His body, we are reflectors of the Light. Just as John the Baptist was not the light, but came to bear witness of the light, so the church is not the light but the witness to the light (John 1:4-9). The incarnate Christ was the Light of the World while He was in the world. But since He is here through His second body, the church and its members radiate His presence as light. God creates the church for His glory. The church is to reflect His nature and character in doxological splendor and brilliant beauty. Tony Evans states in his book *God's Glorious Church*: "As Christ's body which completes His person on earth, the church also becomes the completion of His presence on earth. Jesus makes His presence known in a special way through the church."[8] When Jesus spoke of the promised gift of the Holy Spirit, He said that He, the Spirit, would glorify Him (John 16:13). Now, this same Spirit is the Spirit of truth and the Spirit of the church which was to tell the truth about the Truth. Certainly, this truth is concerning the Word and the written word about the Word. However, the incarnate Word is manifested in the reincarnated word, the body of Christ, communicating through corporate and individual witness the truth about Jesus (Acts 1:8; 2 Corinthians 3:18).

For the sake of Christ's body, we must engage in body life. Since we are members of His body, we must all be responsible to one another. Nurturing is an imperative for the health of the body to the glory of God and the edification of the body (Ephesians 4:16).

Jesus is the focus of Scripture. The Bible, from Genesis to Revelation, is about Him. There is no clear understanding of God without Him, and certainly no right relationship with the Father except through Him. It is through His incarnation that we know the Father; it is also through the Incarnation that humanity can be reconciled to the Father. To redeem man, He had to become man, substituting for humanity on the cross. Disjointed man is restored and a new humanity which includes the church, is established. Through the glorious church, Jews and Gentiles became one "new man." Paul called this new man the reconciled community (2 Corinthians 5:17-21; Ephesians 3:6).

Christ, the head of the church, has no contemporaries. He is without peers. He stands alone as the most pivotal individual to have ever lived on the planet. For there is no other name given under heaven whereby one can be saved from the wrath of God (Acts 4:12). Only Christ can emphatically announce His exclusivity (John 14:6).

Just as Jesus Christ is crucial, pivotal, and exclusive, so is His church, His second body. It is the ignorance of the importance of the church as the bodily presence of Christ on earth that gives impetus to this book. It is my desire that each member of the body of Christ view their union with Christ and one another as an awesome stewardship. This metaphorical language, "body of Christ," is germane only to the New Testament. The term *body of Christ* is the most used term for the church used in the New Testament. Body life language is so true to the reality of the organism. As Peter said, "*we are living stones*" (1 Peter 2:5, ESV). It bespeaks of a spiritual reality between Christ and members of His church. The term *body of Christ* is most appropriate to body life, and relationships to the Head and members of the body. What a wonderful metaphor for this spiritual reality! We are organically joined together forming the body of Christ, also known as the one man, the new humanity, and the new creation (Ephesians 2:11-18). This passage convicts us when we observe the ethnic separations in our churches. The point that Paul is making here is that we are one new man in principle, but are we in practice? It is through our ethnocentrism and denominationalism that we hinder the principle from being practiced.

Healthy churches develop out of a sense of being members one of another for the purpose of being the reincarnated Christ on earth. Here again, the purpose of the book is to encourage and engage the reader in actively living in union with Christ and one another for the sake of the body of Christ. If the church could ever comprehend and conform to God's intention for its presence in the world, we would truly turn the world right side up. The unhealthiness of the body of Christ is not found in the head but rather in the members. Members not in concert with the will of the Head and disjointed from one another will cause the body to be paralytic. Abuse and misuse in the body of Christ as in marriage stems from relational ignorance. We just do not understand the mystery, miracle, and mission of this oneness.

Marriage is designed by God to be a picture, better yet a microcosm of the church of Christ. The oneness in the body of Christ is tantamount to the oneness in marriage. The primary purpose of marriage is to demonstrate Christ's relationship with His church. As the church is one body with many members, marriage is two people becoming one marital person in the "one flesh" relationship. This is the teaching set forth in Ephesians chapter 5, the husband and wife, like Christ and His church, form one person. Listen to Paul as he discusses the marital relationship:

> *"In the same way husbands should love their wives as their own bodies. He who loves his wife loves himself. For no one ever hated his own flesh, but nourishes and cherishes it, just as Christ does the church, because we are members of his body. Therefore, a*

> *man shall leave his father and mother and hold fast to his wife, and the two shall become one flesh. This mystery is profound, and I am saying that it refers to Christ and the church. However, let each one of you love his wife as himself, and let the wife see that she respects her husband"* (Ephesians 5:28-33, ESV).

So, we see the correlation between Christ, His church, and the husband and his wife. Although marriage does not continue in heaven, it points to the marriage between Christ and His church that will continue beyond time into eternity. When divorce occurs in marriages it contradicts the reality of Christ's relationship with His church. The witness of oneness in the body of Christ is hindered by marital divorce. If marriages and churches are to be healthy, each person in marriage and each member in the church should be well and grow in wholeness. I speak of marriage/family because the local congregation consists of this primary institution. Unhealthy families render the local church unhealthy. In a world that militates against marriage and family, the church must be proactive, better yet, pre-active in preparing children, youth and young adults for purposeful marriage and family ministry. In fact, the family must become the primary place in making, marking, maturing, and multiplying disciples for Christ and His church. Church leaders and their families must become the paragon of making, marking, maturing, and multiplying disciples for Christ and His church. Oneness in the body of Christ will always be a challenge as members grow from immaturity to maturity, but healthy leaders equipping the saints for the work of ministry will enable the body to be healthy. No wonder, Paul admonished the Ephesian elders: *"Therefore take heed to yourselves and to all the flock, among which the Holy Ghost hath made you overseers, to feed the church of God, which he hath purchased with his own blood"* (Acts 20:28, NKJV). These pastors were to pay strict attention to their private and public lives, for they had the full attention of the devil, the flesh, and the world. Church leaders today are under constant attack of the enemies of Christ and His church. Fallen pastors and preachers cannot edify the body of Christ in the midst of their fallenness. While the fallen are redeemable, they can do irreparable damage if they attempt to succeed without repentance (see 1 Timothy 5:19-20; Galatians 6:1-5).

In body life, we are called to correspond to our calling as put forth by the apostle Paul. Listen to him:

> *"I, therefore, the prisoner of the Lord, beseech you to walk worthy of the calling with which you were called, with all lowliness and gentleness, with longsuffering, bearing with one another in love, endeavoring to keep the unity of the Spirit in the bond of peace"* (Ephesians 4:1-3, NKJV).

The apostle has spent three chapters setting forth the believer's identity and position in Christ. Because of Jesus our blessed Savior, we are privileged people. Paul opens the first chapter of Ephesians reminding them and us by saying, *"Blessed be the God and Father of our Lord Jesus, who has blessed us with every spiritual blessing in the heavenly places in Christ, just as He chose us in Him before the foundation of the world, that we should be holy and without blame before Him in love, having predestined us to adoption as sons by Jesus Christ himself, according to the good pleasure of His will, to the praise of the glory of His grace, by which He made us accepted in the Beloved"* (Ephesians 1:3-6, NKJV). This long sentence is packed with wonderful who-nesses and where-nesses. It commences with God's unfolding purpose in Christ on behalf of us for His glory. Chapter 4 begins with calling for the Christian to balance his position with his practice. The "therefore" in chapter 4:1 and the personal pronoun, suggest that Paul himself is an example of balancing his walk with his calling.

Paul was not only an example of a Christian living in correspondence to his calling, but he modeled the consequence of such a life. He said he was the *"prisoner of the Lord Jesus Christ."* The call to salvation is not only a call from imprisonment, but to imprisonment. To miss this truth is to render the Christian and the church ineffective in ministry. There are privileges in being in Christ, and there are responsibilities—a prisoner of the Lord Jesus Christ. Could it be that Christians are seldom prisoners for Christ because they do not see themselves as prisoner of Christ? Not seeing yourself as a prisoner of Christ probably is the result of faulty doctrine concerning the lordship of Christ. Right teaching is essential for right behavior and living. Have you ever been locked out or locked in because you lived as prisoner of the Lord Jesus? Have you ever been abandoned and abhorred because you have surrendered your freedom and live in obedience to your Lord? Paul identified himself as one in custody for the sake of Christ. He had been apprehended (Philippians 3:12). The Lord had arrested him on the Road to Damascus, and ever since that day, he had been a prisoner of the Lord Jesus Christ. Perhaps, we prefer to be identified as a preacher, pal, pastor, prophet, parishioner, or priest of Jesus Christ, but Paul saw himself as a prisoner of Christ.

In the third chapter of Ephesians, we discover why Paul was in prison for Christ. He was pressed by the mystery of God. The mystery hidden, but now revealed through Paul's ministry to the Gentiles, bringing both Jews and Gentiles into one body in Christ. Thus, chapter 4 contains the call for us to walk worthy, which is the effectual call unto salvation; but this chapter includes, what I believe is the broader context of this letter, a call into the body of Christ. We are called out of the world into a new relationship with Christ and other believers. John R. W. Stott stated, "Through Jesus Christ, who died for sinners and was raised from death, God is creating something entirely new, not just new life for individuals but a new society. Paul sees an alienated humanity being reconciled; a fractured humanity being created. It is a magnificent vision."[9] The call to Christ is also a call to live together in His body. To respond to Him and to reject membership in His body through the local congregation places some doubt upon one's response in salvation. For the call to faith in Christ is a call to fellowship with fellow believers who share common life in Christ. While we believe that the local church membership is not necessarily membership in the invisible body of Christ, it is a reflection of our new relationship with Christ that includes our relationship with other believers. For one to attempt to embrace the invisible and avoid membership in the visible is living contrary to the New Testament model, as we have aforementioned (Acts 2:42-47). A churchless Christianity is a dysfunctional and disjointed Christianity. How can a Christian demonstrate being members one of another in isolation of others? The powerful metaphor of the "body of Christ" transcends the idea that Christians are only members of the invisible church. There is no such teaching in the New Testament. One evidential mark of our salvation is our love for our brothers and sisters (1 John 3:14), which is a mark that can only be manifested in community. We just cannot love disconnected from other members of the family of God. Although it challenges us in the one anotherness, let us remember that love calls us to be inconvenienced (1 Corinthians 13; 1 John 4:7-21).

Although the calling of salvation is personal, it is also lived out interpersonally. As forestated, remember we are birthed into the kingdom of which the church is a colony of that kingdom. We are fellows in the fellowship of body life and citizenship of the redeemed society (see John 3:5-7; Ephesians 2:19-22). This is the fellowship that Paul states we must walk worthy of in Ephesians 4:1-2; and do so *"with all humility and gentleness, with patience, bearing with one another in love, eager to maintain the unity of the Spirit in the bond of peace."* For the sake of body life, members are to relate to one another in lowliness. This quality runs counter to the thinking of this world. This world encourages pride and self-assertiveness. Humility, like meekness, is viewed as weakness. The world's idea is that you will never get ahead being humble. This world promotes pride in the place of humility. To be lowly was ignoble in Greek and the Roman world in Paul's day. It was despised and so is it today. When Christianity is at its best, it is contradistinctive from the world. Proverbs reminds us, *"Pride goes before destruction, and a haughty spirit before a fall. Better to be of a humble spirit with the lowly, than to divide the spoil with the proud"* (Proverbs 16:18-19, NKJV). Pride is sin, and, as a matter of fact, it was the first sin. It is the foundation of all sins. Faith and repentance in salvation is turning from self-assertion and independence to surrendering self to Christ as Lord and Savior. The crucified life that Paul talks about in Galatians, *"I have been crucified with Christ; it is no longer I who live, but Christ lives in me; and the life which I now live in the flesh I live by faith in the Son of God, who loved me and gave himself for me,"* (Galatians 2:20, NKJV) is a life humbled before the Lord Jesus. Jesus said, *"If anyone desires to come after Him, let him deny himself, and take up His cross, and follow Him"* (Matthew 16:24, NKJV). Humbleness before God in salvation enables humility in association with one another in the body of Christ. The meek mentioned in (Matthew 5:5) speaks of being broken. It is the taming of the wildness in the believer to the point of submission under the Lord Jesus Christ. The believer, after encountering Jesus as Lord, is prepared to live in the body of Christ in mutual submission (Ephesians 5:21). Hear this: *"Do nothing from selfish ambition or conceit, but in humility count others more significant than yourselves. Let each of you look not only to his own interests, but also to the interests of others"* (Philippians 2:3-4, NKJV). According to Philippians 2:5-8, Jesus is the paragon of humility. And having His nature or life makes manifesting lowliness in the body of Christ possible.

While we operate from submission to Christ in salvation, being humble is still a challenge for us. It remains a challenge because of the presence of the flesh that is the epitome of self-centeredness. John MacArthur states, "Humility is a virtue to be highly sought, but never claimed, because once claimed it is forfeited."[10] To be preoccupied with being humble can lead to manipulating humility when it should be manifested in the power of the Holy Spirit. When you think you are humble and call yourself humble you are probably not being humble. Others should testify to your humility. False humility is pride disguising itself in humility. True humility is coming to the end of self. It is the result of self-denial and being filled with the Holy Spirit. Where there is true humility, there is no deception concerning your unworthiness, and there is an awareness of grace. In humility you are fully aware that it is all about Christ and His church, to His glory and edification of others at your expense. Again, let me quote John MacArthur: "Humility allows us to see ourselves as we are, because it shows us before God as He is. Just as pride is behind every conflict we have with other people and every problem of fellowship we have with the Lord, so humility is behind every harmonious human relationship, every spiritual success, and every moment of joyous fellowship with the Lord."[11] Also awareness of our interdependence in the body of Christ should humble us. We live and serve for the sake of the body of Christ and not self-edification.

Meekness is another moral quality ensuring unity in the body of Christ. Meekness or gentleness is related to humbleness (lowliness). It helps to clarify the true nature of being humble. It seems wrong to have a poor opinion of yourself, your power, and your faculties, suggesting low self-esteem, nonetheless humility requires it. But meekness, which is also understood by some as weakness, helps us to see that weakness is strength under control for the sake of others in the body of Christ. So, it is in humility, for the sake of the body that one is busy esteeming others, appearing as a servant, and not a king, fully aware that you are sons of God. There is no better example of this than seen in the "kenosis" statement of Paul concerning Jesus: *"Who, being in the very form of God, did not consider it robbery to be equal with God, but made Himself of no reputation, taking the form of a bondservant, and coming in the likeness of men. And being found in appearance as a man, humbled Himself and became obedient to the point of death, even the death of the cross"* (Philippians 2:6-8, NKJV). If our salvation is a matter of Jesus' humanity and humiliation, surely relationship in the body of Christ ought to be coming to the end of ourselves.

In Jesus of Nazareth, we have the supreme example of humility and meekness. And these qualities must be experienced in the body of Christ, if we are to have unity beyond principle seen in practice. Jesus has supreme worth as the Son of God, as the King of Kings, and as the Lord of Lords. But He made Himself sin without sinning—a servant unto death for our sakes. Yes, His worth was within Himself, but He surrendered His divine prerogatives to reconcile us into Himself, giving us worth in our union with Him. Before sin, man had worth, created in the image of God, but, in sin, the image was severely marred in the first Adam and restored in the Second Adam through His cross (see Ephesians 2:13; Roman 3:23). To speak of self-esteem and self-worth apart from Christ is humanistic at best and idolatry at worst. This way we celebrated and congratulated *"the poor in spirit"* (Matthew 5:3, NKJV), which are those who are bankrupt in spirit and understand their utter need for a Savior. They understand their helplessness and their hopelessness. They realize that they are not self-sufficient. In Christ, we have worth, but in the body, we must have a servant opinion of ourselves. This poor opinion of ourselves, of our powers and faculties, is thinking and acting like servants in the body of Christ. Humility and meekness are both elusive, for it is natural for us to want to be served. The mother of Zebedee's sons wanted her two sons to have privilege in the kingdom and rule over others in the kingdom. However, Jesus informed her by contrasting the world with the kingdom when He said to her: *"You know that the rulers of the Gentiles lord over them, and their high official exercise authority over them. Not so with you. Instead, whoever wants to become great among you must be your servant, and whoever wants to be first must become your slave—just as the Son of Man did not come to be served, but to serve, and to give His life a ransom of many"* (Matthew 20:25-28, NIV).

It is natural to want to rule over others, but it is supernatural to want to serve others. Everyone desires the title, but few desires to take up the towel. Here are these two terms, humility and meekness, gentleness of the strong, whose strength is under control. Dr. Stott says, "It is the quality of a strong personality who is nevertheless master of himself and the servant of others."[12] Behind almost every discord is pride, and concord comes from having the qualities of humility and meekness.

Unity in the body of Christ also requires that we are longsuffering and forbearing with one another in love. As humility and meekness are coupled together, so is longsuffering and forbearing. In longsuffering (patience) members of the body are holding out in their minds before giving room for action. Forbearing is holding up under a load of vexations piled upon by another member of the body. All this is done within love which is seeking God's best for the other brother or sister in Christ. It is not eternal suffering or forbearance, for that would not be love, because when love is no longer able to pursue its purpose of achieving God's best for the other through these two virtues, some type of discipline may be the next step (see Matthew 18:15-20; Revelation 3:19; Hebrews 12:5-6). To experience unity in the body there are things we must learn to put up with, bear, endure, and suffer through in an attempt to understand each other. This may necessitate cultivating relationships with people you would rather distance yourself from. But remember you cannot afford to do so, for you are organically related (1 Corinthians 12:21a). Patience and forbearance are personal qualities used in interpersonal relationships for the health of the body of Christ. What I mean is that we exercise these qualities in loving involvement with those who vex us. It is living with mutual tolerance with one another. We must remember that God did not love us from long distance (see John 1:14; Romans 5:8). He came to us in order to relate to us, and then to die for us. His love for us was not passive, but an aggressive love. Christ proved in the Incarnation that you and I cannot truly love others without being involved in their lives one way or another.

Love is the final quality mentioned in the paragraph. It is really the context out of which the others come. Love is the nature of God, supremely expressed in Jesus' grace act on Calvary. It is the love that is spread abroad in the hearts of the believer (Romans 5:5). This love that each member of the body possesses is from another country—it is *agape*. Unconditional love expressed in grace toward the undeserved and unmerited, is love rooted in the very nature of God (1 John 4:8). The depth of God's love is wonderfully defined through His moral nature. His holiness and righteousness contextualized in His justice and wrath gives glorious definition to His love. Truly, God did "so love the world" (John 3:16). What a love! This love of God which is who He is, is also who we are as members of Christ's body (see 1 John 4:7-21) corporately and individually. According to the apostle Paul, in the body we are unified by this love (see Colossians 3:12-14). We love in the body of Christ when we esteem others higher than ourselves and have strength under control for the sake of others; when we are patient when offended by others, and when we endure while wronged by others. Each of these four virtues are expressions of love, and Jesus in His life on earth demonstrated His love for us in all four of these qualities. He humbled Himself to the level of servant (see Philippians 2:6-8). In His meekness, He demonstrated strength under control (see 2 Corinthians 13:4; Matthew 26:52-53). He demonstrated patience and forbearance (see Isaiah 53:1-12). He demonstrated His love (see Romans 5:6-11).

The call to maintain unity in the body of Christ is a reminder that we cannot create unity. We can only maintain unity. The call is for believers to act like who they are in the body of Christ and to walk worthy of the calling. To be a healthy body, members need to practice the four qualities mentioned. Because everything in this world militates against unity. Christians should make every effort continuously to maintain unity. In an individualistic world, maintaining unity within the body of Christ with diversity of gifts, and in Christendom divided into several denominations, is a challenging enterprise. Still, we must work hard *"to keep the unity of the Spirit in the bond of peace"* (Ephesians 4:3, NIV). This verse is a transitional verse, linking what has been said with what is about to be said. This unity that must be maintained is the result of the Spirit's work and the work of Christ, who won our peace with God through His atoning blood, reconciling us to God and to each other in His body (see Ephesians 2:13-16). The body has been formed. Each member is to maintain the healthy functioning of the one body by living the kind of life that is not self-centered, but Christ-centered, in order to build up the body so that it will become a safe place to become who we are in Christ Jesus.

Body life is the result and expression of the Trinity as seen in Ephesians 4:4-6. This passage delineates the origin and impetus of oneness in the body of Christ and in marriages. Since the entire epistle of Ephesians is about unity, and marriage is a reflection of the church as set forth in chapter 5, we must also include the one flesh principle.

The seven unities in the passage find their origin in the one God who is revealed in three persons. Jesus' prayer for unity has been answered in the birth of the church (John 17:20-23). All believers in the Lord Jesus Christ make up the body of Christ. Each local congregation is a part of the one body. The oneness in Christ is a reality that must be manifested outwardly in order to get the world to believe. The invisible church must become visible to be a witness in the world.

The Christian church must not divide over non-essentials, which often hinders us from maintaining the unity of the Spirit. Christology, *"what think ye of Christ"* (Matthew 22:42), is the essential element of unity. The wrong Jesus will cause disunity in the church, whether or not it is the body of Christ. It is sad to admit, but denominationalism has fractured the oneness in the body. Someone may say, let us then become non-denominational; changing titles and distinctions will not help us to manifest oneness, for even the non-denominational churches have become denominations. We must learn to accept diversities in the body of Christ. Different forms of worship styles, preaching styles, cultural distinctions, and giftedness are not enemies to oneness if there is unity of the faith (Ephesians 4:13-15). If we have the right Jesus and Christ, Jesus Himself says "amen" through revealed Scripture; there can be oneness (Matthew 16:13-20). The Nicene Creed helps us to articulate the right Jesus:

> *"We believe in one God, the Father almighty, maker of heaven and earth, of all things visible and invisible.*
>
> *And in one Lord Jesus Christ, the only Son of God, begotten from the Father before all ages, God from God, light from light, true God from true God, begotten, not made: of the same essence as the Father. Through him all things were made. For us and for our salvation he came down from heaven; he became incarnate by the Holy Spirit and the Virgin Mary and was made human. He was crucified for us under Pontius Pilate; he suffered and was buried. The third day he rose again, according to the Scriptures. He ascended to heaven and is seated at the right hand of the Father. He will come again with glory to judge the living and the dead. His kingdom will never end.*
>
> *And we believe in the Holy Spirit, the Lord, the giver of life. He proceeds from the Father and the Son, and with the Father and the Son is worshipped and glorified. He spoke through the prophets. We believe in one holy catholic and apostolic church. We affirm one baptism for the forgiveness of sins. We look forward to the resurrection of the dead, and to life in the world to come. Amen."*[13]

Peter's Pentecostal sermon sets forth the right Jesus to this Jewish audience (Acts 2:22-36) whom some became primal members of the body of Christ. Earlier, Peter had given hearsay accounts when Jesus inquired about what people were saying about who He was. But Jesus does not want those who would be charter members of this new body to rely on information, but inspiration; so, He asked Peter, *"Who do you say that I am?"* (Matthew 16:16, ESV). Peter spoke up: *"You are the Christ, the Son of the living God"* (Matthew 16:16, ESV).

The church is only the body of Christ when our Christology is according to Scripture alone. Christianity leans on no other sources than the Bible. There may be other documents and disciplines of history that correspond to Scripture concerning Christ and His church. However, the Jesus Christ of Scripture alone, as rightly divided through proper interpretation, is the Head and Chief Cornerstone of His church (2 Timothy 2:15). Therefore wrong Jesus Christ, wrong church.

The church from her inception has fought from within, heresies that threaten the health and life of Christ and His church. One such heresy comes from a fourth-century theologian named Arius, who I believe influenced the Jehovah Witness cult. Arius could not accept the teaching that Jesus was the very God. He thought it did damage to monotheism—the belief in one God. Arius saw value in Jesus but only as the first and highest of all created beings, misunderstanding and misinterpreting passages like Colossians 1:15-21, which spoke of first in rank and not chronologically first in creation. However, at the Council of Nicaea, with Athanasius challenging him, Arianism was declared to have the wrong Jesus, and Athanasius declared that Jesus Christ is very God. Arian and his modern-day followers, in their attempt to be monotheist, become polytheistic, claiming that Jesus is a lesser god who created the universe, which is also Gnostic thought. Thus, if Jesus is creator, he is a lesser god. These heretics cannot handle the mystery of God in His Trinitarian reality revealed in Scripture (see John 1:1-18; 14:9; 20:28 Matthew 28:19, 20; 1 Timothy 3:16). There are others who attempt to explain the unexplainable when they explain the mystery as God playing three different roles (modalism or tritheism) or three separate gods (polytheism). The Jesus of modalism and tritheism is the wrong Jesus. This is problematic for those who claim to be members of the body of Christ.

Removal of the reality of the trinity is to deny the reality of the one flesh in Christian marriage, and the one body of Christ. In marriage two people become one marital person, reflecting the truth found in the trinity. In the church, many members form one body in Christ. Both of these mysteries celebrate monotheism in light of the Trinity (Ephesians 5:28-33). The mystery that Paul refers to is primarily the church, but it is clear that he views the one flesh in marriage as mystery also. As Jews and Gentiles form one new man, so does the husband-and-wife form one marital person. As in the Trinity, the husband and wife remain two distinct persons as the Father, the Son, and Holy Spirit are distinct. So, in the church, the many members are distinct individuals forming one new man, the second body of Christ.

Unity of the faith is also important to unity in the body of Christ, as aforementioned, especially when it comes to the essentials. According to Ephesians 4:5, there is oneness in "one Lord, one faith, and one baptism." Living under the Lordship of Christ will certainly help us to maintain unity in the body. Where there is common faith, doctrinally speaking, practical unity can be experienced. When physical baptism in water reminds of our common salvation described in Romans 6 and spoken of in Jude 3, unity in the body in practice can be realized. There is a general testimony in the act of baptism. *"For all of us have been baptized into Christ Jesus were baptized into his death, were buried by baptism into death, and raised from the dead by the glory of the Father, walking in newness of life—common life"* (Romans 6:3-4—personal emphasis). Spirit baptism is not in view here, but it also causes oneness more than water baptism (1 Corinthians 12:12-13). We have spoken of this in the previous chapter. Now, the one God and Father is the means of our unity and the context of our unity, as Lord, and empowers all, in power, indwells all, in His presence, causes unity.

Oneness in the body is the result of having one Lord. There is only one Head of the church. This truth is disturbing when local churches are going in different directions, saying they are following Jesus. It appears that Jesus is schizophrenic, because the one body seems to be disjointed and not univocal in purpose. Jesus is Lord of His church. Therefore, the last thing Jesus said ought not to be the least thing the church of Jesus Christ engages in (Matthew 28:16-20).

What finally unites us is our common hope. One common personal goal is Christ formed in us. The mark, we press towards is not heaven, but conforming to the image of God's dear Son. This eschatological hope started in justification, continues through sanctification, and consummates in glorification. It is the impetus for oneness in the body, for it is the destiny of every member in the body of Christ (see Romans 8:29; Galatians 4:19; Philippians 3:12-14; Colossians 1:28). This common hope is not an elusive hope, but a sure one, guaranteed through the work and presence of the Holy Spirit (see 2 Corinthians 5:5; Ephesians 1:11-14).

Commonality has been our focus in body life; now we turn to diversities in the body. We go from what all of us have, to what each of us have. We are the same in nature, but like the Trinity and marriage, we differ in function. Sameness is uninteresting and lifeless uniformity. It does not project the dynamic life of diversity in the body.

In Ephesians 4:7-12, the grace given us is not saving grace, but enabling serving grace. Saving grace is poured out on us, it is lavished on us; enabling—serving grace is measured, proportionally distributed. Dr. Stott says, "The unity of the church is due to Charis, God's grace having reconciled us himself; but the diversity of the church is due to charismata, God's gifts distributed to church members."[14]

The gifting of the church is the work of the Trinity. It all starts with the Father giving the gift of His Son (John 3:16), the Son giving the gift of His life (Mark 10:45), Jesus giving the gift of eternal life to believers (John 10:28), the Father and the Son giving the gift of the Holy Spirit to believers (John 14:26; 16:7), and each person of the Trinity giving gifts to the church. In Ephesians 4, the Son; in Romans 12, the Father; in 1 Corinthians 12, the Holy Spirit. It is clear that the gifting of the church is the operation of the Trinity. In truth, the distinct persons of the Trinity never work in isolation of one another.

Here in Ephesians 4, Jesus is the gift giver. He bestows gifts to His church after He is triumphant through His cross and resurrection, and now seated at the place of authority in heaven. The first thing He does at the position of authority is to equip His church, His new body on earth, with gifted leaders. Christ first gives gifted persons: apostles, prophets, evangelists and pastors/teachers. The first two are pioneer leaders, foundational to the church. The apostles referred to in the passage are apostles in the primary sense. They are referred to with the prophets as the foundation of the early church (Ephesians 2:20-22). They are foundational in the sense of their message and not who they were. The church does not rest on them, but on Christ the Chief Cornerstone. However, the apostles were the first and the prophets were the second gifted persons given to the church (1 Corinthians 12:28).

In the secondary sense, every Christian who is sent (John 17:18; 20:21) is an apostle or missionary. An apostle of the church is a missionary sent by the church (2 Corinthians 8:23). But the apostle of Christ is directly sent by Him (Acts 1:21-26) and were witnesses to the Resurrection. Also, Ephesians 4:11, more than likely refers to apostles in the primary sense. In Acts 15:22-23, is an example of apostles of the church. Galatians 1:1 gives us a clue to who are Christ's apostles. The apostles in the primary sense and the secondary sense depends on who is the sender, Christ or the church. Also, evidence of the primary apostles were signs and wonders (see Mark 3:13-19; 2 Corinthians 12:12).

Prophets were also foundational, gifted men who received direct revelation from God. They are listed second to the apostles and are distinct from the general idea of preaching God's Word. Christ gave some, not all, to be apostles and prophets. It is the business of all believers to prophesy. Preaching must not be seen as the prerogative of a few, but the priority of all (Acts 8:1-4). However, in Ephesians 4:11, these were gifted men who were gifts to the church. In the church you would have believers who had the gift of prophecy, but Ephesians 4:11 references to the office of the prophet and his revelatory message. Here again, the prophets mentioned here are foundational and primary in church history. In Acts 2, the demonstrated prophesy is the same as the gifted men of Ephesians 4:11. The prophesying in Acts 2 would be testimonial in nature, a witnessing to their experience of salvation. Much of Joel's promise of prophesying would come to fruition in the eschaton. The prophet, you should know did not always speak a new revelation, but expounded on what God had already revealed. The apostles and the prophets were foundational gifts, and once the foundation is laid there are no successors. Thus, there are none in the primary sense. Only in the secondary sense are there apostles and prophets serving as missionaries, evangelists, and preachers. Evangelists are gifted men given to the church. This also is a distinct group of men for not everyone in the church is set apart as an evangelist. But everyone is to engage in evangelism. An evangelist proclaims the Gospel, while this is the business of the entire church, we are told that *"he gave some to be evangelist"* (Ephesians 4:11, NKJV). I think the distinction is vividly seen in the ministries of Jonathan Edwards. George Whitfield, Charles Finney, Dwight L. Moody, R. A. Torrey, Billy Graham. Evangelists are gifted men, particularly set apart for this work. Some see Bishop T. D. Jakes as the apparent heir to Billy Graham, but I am not so sure. Jakes' gathering cannot be classified as evangelistic in nature. It is more inspirational. What we have today are mostly internal revivals. Evangelists are certainly needed these days. But the pure evangelist, who focuses on preaching the Gospel to the world of unsaved persons as a way of life, is rare. There are the pastor/evangelists, but not the fulltime evangelist, dedicated to the ministry to the lost. The apostle Paul urged Timothy to do the work of an evangelist (2 Timothy 4:5). It is thought that Timothy and Titus were pastors. Some believe, Timothy was the bishop of the church in Ephesus. He is certainly addressed in the Pastoral Epistles as the recipient. The work of the evangelist, planting churches of new believers, is the mandate to the Savior (Matthew 28:19, 20).

The last gifted persons given by Christ to the church are pastors/teachers. The absence of the definite article and comma before the conjunction "and" suggest that pastors are teachers. Their main task is to feed the flock (Acts 20:28). The pastor is the primary teacher in the church. All other teachers and teachings should line-up with his proclamation of biblical truth. He does so by rightly dividing and demonstrating the Word of Truth, laboring hard in the communication of the Word of God (see 2 Timothy 2:15; 4:2; 1 Timothy 5:17). The pastor is a gift with gifts to the church. He is a noun gift with the gift to communicate the Word of God. He guards, he feeds the church as shepherd. He oversees each member's journey towards the image of Jesus Christ (Hebrews 13:7, 17). As elder, he is spiritually mature, enabling him to be a pioneer of the faith.

We started this paragraph of Scripture with the announcement that each one in the body of Christ has been graced with gifts. The Paul turns immediately to the gifted leaders who are gifts to the church in order to equip the church for the work of ministry. All of the gifted men are engaged in communicating the Word of God. This indicates that the health and growth of the body depends on the teaching and preaching ministries. When we look at churches that place more emphasis on the lesser gifts, like the sign gifts, there is no wonder, we are producing, an audience and not an army for Christ and His church. Spiritual gifts are important for the church to fulfill its primary purpose, building up the members into the image of Christ. John MacArthur says, "Spiritual gifts are the Lord's primary channel of making Christians to become Christ in the world, His visible and manifest body."[15] His definition of spiritual gifts is most comprehensive: "spiritual gifts are divine enablement's for ministry, characteristics of Jesus Christ that are to be manifested through the body corporate, just as they were manifested through the body incarnate."[16] If the purpose of spiritual gifts is for the church to become Christ's presence in the world, it is crucial that the church operate in the power of the Holy Spirit.

The diversity in the body of Christ is not the same as division in the body. Diversity is constructive and division is destructive. Christ designed church unity to function in diversity, and Satan's scheme is to disrupt unity through division.

The problems in the Corinthian church were regarding gifts, among other things. Paul's response gives us insight and vital information on how oneness and diversity can exist in the same body. Much of the division in the Corinthian church was due to ignorance. The saints were confusing their past associations with ecstatic experiences in the flesh with the spiritual operation of the Holy Spirit. They probably viewed being out of control as the Holy Spirit's doing. However, whenever there is an out-of-control situation, it is not of the Spirit (1 Corinthians 14:15, 33, 40). They were comparing their pagan experiences with the Holy Spirit's manifestation of some gifts. They were rich in spiritual gifts, but ignorant concerning their function and operations in the church. The mystery religions, from whence they came, operated from a kind of frenzy atmosphere. Emotionalism can be dangerous. A lot of what we call spiritual in the church is mere emotional expressions rooted in some cultures. We must not deny the emotional element of our personalities, however, emotions should be the response of truth worship. Spirited worship is not always spiritual worship. Jesus said we should *"worship in spirit and truth"* (John 4:24, NKJV). The point that I am attempting to make is that spiritual ignorance causes the misuse of spiritual gifts, and, therefore, hinders unity in diversity.

The evidence of spiritual gifts is found in doctrine and not experience. And the doctrine of Christology is crucial. *"What think ye of Christ and whose Son is He"* (Matthew 22:42) is necessary in the Spirit's functioning in the church. There is a danger in the church of emphasizing the Holy Spirit with no reference to Jesus Christ. Jesus as the second Person of the Trinity is uniquely important. The right God is determined by who is His Son, and the right move of the Spirit is determined by who the Holy Spirit speaks of (John 16:13-15). Therefore, any teaching that does not view Jesus correctly is not of the Spirit (1 Corinthians 12:3). When one curses Jesus, it is not of the Spirit, when one confesses Jesus as Lord, it is of the Spirit. Confessing Jesus as Lord is saying, He is God and is all sufficient. In salvation, the Holy Spirit is not the focus, the Son is. The Spirit is the agent in regeneration, but Christ is the focus (Colossians 1:19).

In 1 Corinthians 12:4, we notice that this unity is contextualized in the Trinity. We see the Trinity involvement in the gifting of the church where there are diversities of gifts, and the same Spirit; differences of ministries, and the same Lord; and diversities of activities, and the same God who works all in all. Herein, is the purpose of the Holy Spirit in each member for the profit of the corporate body. There is no room for pride and one-upmanship in the body. Bragging and comparing gifts or feeling inferior has no place in the church. The one who gives the gifts, and who also enables their use, is manifested in each member. Diversity is found in the fact that each member is gifted, and unity comes from the same Spirit in each member for the purpose of building up the one body.

Gifts are given for the common good of all members of the body. They are not by any means give for private use and edification. Whenever and wherever gifts are used privately, it is considered misuse of God-given gifts. Private use does not fit the corporate purpose of gifts. To understand this key to the operation of gifts is necessary to body life. Private somewhat negates corporate life of the body. The Lord Jesus Christ enables every member of the body through their gifs to manifest Himself in the church and in the world (1 Corinthians 12:7). John MacArthur makes this observation: "The church is to be Christ in the world. I have chosen to call the church, 'body II' and the incarnation, 'body I'—Christ in a human body. We are body II—Christ alive in the world in the church. This is a vital reality that we have to understand. The Lord Jesus wanted to remain in the world after the ascension by reproducing in us His very essence, life, personality, and character, so that we might manifest Christ to the world."[17] Gifted men have been given to equip each member to serve in order to build up the body of Christ (Ephesians 4:12).

In Ephesians 4:7 and 1 Peter 4:10-11, the diversity of gifts is declared; but in 1 Corinthians 12 and Romans 12, the diversity of gifts is delineated. And then their function is illustrated through the symbolism of the human body (1 Corinthians 12:14-27). Our giftedness is according to the will of God (1 Corinthians 12:11, 18, 22). Paul, in Ephesians, states that we are "*fitly joined together*" (Ephesians 4:16, NIV). We are not uniformed bricks, rather individual stones of different shapes fitted together in one edifice. Therefore, it is unbiblical to seek gifts, they are given according to the will and purpose of God. Having the gift of the Spirit guarantees our giftedness in the body of Christ. The best we can do is to surrender our will to the Holy Spirit and develop our gifts through the knowledge of the Word of God to properly use our gifts to edify the body of Christ. May I quote again Dr. MacArthur: "Each of us who knows the Lord Jesus Christ is an individual and vital member of that body. And, like members of the human body, we must work together in order to bring about a full, functioning body. The church, in the same way, must have a mutual ministering and working interdependence for the purpose of unity in body II. God would then be visible through the manifestation of Christ in the corporate life of the church."[18]

Body life happens when there is growth through interpersonal relationships in the body (Ephesians 4:12-16). Leaders are placed in the church for the purpose of equipping members to grow through interpersonal relationships. The word *equip* carries the idea of mending nets (Matthew 4:21). When Jesus found some of His disciples, they were busy mending nets for they were fishermen. At that time, they did not know that their secular profession would become the spiritual ministry. If the fisherman is to be successful in catching fish, the nets must be mended and cleaned. Cleansing the nets is not the focus here, but is relevant to the catching of fish, because unclean nets will deter fish from getting into the net. However, the emphasis here is on mending nets in order to catch the fish. Jesus called the disciples to follow Him, and He informed them that their obedience would result in becoming fishers of men (Matthew 4:19). Let me mention, parenthetically, that I believe Jesus meant for His disciples to focus on men in particular. The disciples' objective in following Jesus would change from fish to men. The word *equip* also carries the idea of setting dislocated bones. Both ideas denote relationships. The building of the church would happen through mending—"perfecting the saints," and "binding saints" to minister to each other.

If the church is to be effective in reaching men for Christ, there must be the mending of relationships and setting dislocated members back in place. body life is a net, working together for the purpose of attracting and catching men for Christ. It takes each strand of rope to form a net to catch fish. It takes each member, functioning as placed in the body, to effective evangelizing the world.

Edifying the body is to grow numerically and incarnationally. We grow from the inside out, which is the safe way of growing the church. Mature Christians become midwives in the growth process. When churches grow from the outside in, they are not properly prepared to sustain the growth. Healthy churches are the best context for growing new believers. Therefore, spiritual formation should precede numerical growth. Children should be born into functional families. It is rare that healthy children come from dysfunctional families. So, it is in the church. Mended relationships—washing nets (Luke 5:2)—creates an atmosphere for sinners to believe in Jesus, and then grow in grace knowledge (John 13:34-35).

The mending or equipping is primarily accomplished through the preaching and teaching of the Word of God. Proper Christian discipleship will affect evangelism. Churches grow through the Word, not music and programs, but the Word (2 Timothy 3:16-17). Let me remind us that the goal of leaders and teachers is to lead and teach believers, so that they can be conformed to the image of Christ (Romans 8:29; Galatians 4:19). Equipping believers to build up the body is done first and foremost by developing them towards the image of Jesus. The Gospel must be first demonstrated and then proclaimed as the whole body proclaims the Gospel through a dynamic changed life (1 Peter 2:9). Therefore, the means of growing through interpersonal relationships commences with discipleship, and then corporate and individual evangelism.

The methodology for affecting interpersonal relationship in the body is by leading each member toward unity of the faith and of the knowledge of the Son of God, speaking the truth in love (Ephesians 4:13-15). Remember, the unity is positional, but it must be maintained practically. Our invisible being needs to become visible. We are one body. Now, let us act like it. Each member of the body needs to grow up in order that this one new man (corporate church) might express the fullness of Christ on earth (Ephesians 4:13).

By unity of the faith, we speak of the body of doctrinal truth. We have already discussed faith that leads to salvation, and positional unity, but now we speak of faith that leads to practical unity in the body. Doctrinal ignorance keeps the visible church from expressing oneness. As God is one, so is His truth. There may be levels of the same truth, but there are no different, conflicting truths about God in Christ. Contradictions are not in God's Word. They stem from man's opinions and misinterpretations. Individual experiences should never supersede the objective truth of Scripture. Rather, all experiences should be measured by Scripture. The danger in our day is to view truth as subjective. There is a universalism out there that does not glorify the oneness of God. Some believe, "that all roads lead to God." Others believe that truth is whatever you perceive it to be. Pilate asked Jesus, "*What is truth?*" (John 18:38, NKJV). Jesus had already proclaimed that He was the truth (John 14:6). Truth is fundamentally who and not what. Truth cannot be subjective if Jesus is the center of veracity. Therefore, this unity of the faith is the truth about Jesus, the witness and revelation of God.

The early church grew because of doctrinal teaching. I have heard it said that doctrine divides the church. No! Doctrine is the cohesiveness of the body of Christ (Acts 2:41-42). Unstable Christians and churches are caused by absence of unity of the faith (Ephesians 4:14-16). The most pivotal is the doctrine of Christology. I know have spoken of this before, but it is worthy of reiterating.

We may differ on the mode of baptism, election and free will, polity, practice, spiritual gifts, inherent sin, eternal security, and the second coming of Christ, but we cannot have unity if we have the wrong Christ. Doctrine is never to be an end within itself, but rather a platform to cultivating intimacy with Christ and members of His church. The purpose of doctrine must not be mere cognition. Rather, transformation is the goal and objective of teaching (Philippians 3:10-11). Knowledge mentioned in Ephesians 4:13 is a full knowledge that progressively moves the believer to a robust romance with the Redeemer. Jesus desires to know us intimately (John 10:27). Doctrine should lead the believer into obedience, driven by love and grace. The unity of the faith leads to this experimental knowledge. When believers only grow cognitively, the church is not edified. Each member must be equipped, encouraged, and engaged, and endeavor *"to be conformed to the image of God's Son"* (Romans 8:29, NKJV). The purpose of doctrine/teaching is to *"present everyone mature in Christ"* (Colossians 1:28, ESV).

Paul described marriage between doctrine (the faith) and knowledge (the relationship) as *"speaking the truth in love"* (Ephesians 4:15, NKJV).

Doctrine must be taught with both head and heart. It is designed to know, not only about Jesus, but know Him intimately. Speaking the truth in love does not mean accommodating error (2 Timothy 3:16-17), rather passionately declaring truth that will cause a believer to love God to obedience in repentance when called for.

Individual growth of members in the body causes Christ's fullness in the world. John MacArthur rightly said, "The church in the world is Jesus Christ in the world, because the church is now the fullness of His incarnate body in world."[19] Christ in all of us enables us to be the manifestation of His presence in the world. This is an awesome spiritual reality and an awesome responsibility. Dr. Lloyd Martin Jones spoke of the reality when he wrote, "So I must learn to think of myself, humble unworthy insignificant Christian as I am, as someone who is essential and vital to the fullness of the mystical body of Christ."[20] Dr. Jones saw this awesome reality as a call to holiness which is also the idea to *"walk worthy of the calling with which we have been called"* (Ephesians 4:1, NKJV).

Body life is members engaged in an indispensable union, and this union is vital to the spiritual growth in the body and its members, which makes reconciliation between members and the reclaiming of inactive members of the visible church necessary. Christ did not design a believer to grow separate from the body. No wonder we hear in the admonition, *"Not forsaking the assembling of ourselves together, as is the manner of some, but exhorting one another, and so much the more as you see the Day approaching"* (Hebrews 10:25, NKJV). This indispensable union makes it advantageous that when a member is *"overtaken in any trespass, you who are spiritual restore such a one in a spirit of gentleness, considering yourself lest you also be tempted"* (Galatians 6:1, NKJV). This one anotherness in the body makes it necessary *"that there should be no schism in the body, but that the members should have the same care for one another, and if one member suffers, all the members suffer with it; or if one member is honored, all the members rejoice with it"* (1 Corinthians 12:25-26). The call to love one another is loving self in this mysterious oneness. This is also true in marriage (Ephesians 5:28-31).

Christ has so structured the body according to His purpose and plan. He has placed each member in the body where He wants them to function for His glory. From the Head, His whole body is designed to grow into conformity to Himself (1 Peter 2:5). We are called to be conformed to the Head and Chief Cornerstone. Each member of the body has His nature or life, and we are His corporate witnesses. The power and authority of Christ creates the body, but it is functional and effective as each member depends on the Holy Spirit in the use of gifts in the context of love. Where there is proper use of gifts, there is growth in the body (Ephesians 4:16).

Body life is not the same as a busy and active church. There are well-organized churches with boards, budgets, bylaws, buildings, and busyness that don't function as an organism. It can be an exciting church, an enthusiastic church, an ecstatic church, and emotive, but not function as an organism. Only the Holy Spirit operative in the church can produce functional body life. We know that the life of the body originates from the Head, causing life to flow throughout the body. Dr. D. M. Lloyd Jones mentions that "Christ is the life of the church and if there is no vital relationship to Him there will be no life, and the church will be dead."[21] The life of the body is nurtured as every member cultivates his or her relationship with Christ and each other. Christ is not only the life of the body, His life flows through each member. When hands and feet move without the head, there is dysfunction, epilepsy, and convulsions in the body. There are similarities between body life and Jesus' teaching concerning the vine and the branches. Listen to Jesus: *"Abide in Me, and I in you. As the branch cannot bear fruit of itself, unless it abides in the vine, neither can you unless you abide in Me. I am the vine; you are the branches. He who abides in Me, and I in him, bears much fruit; for without Me you can do nothing"* (John 15:4-5, NKJV). Proper body life is determined by whether or not the life of Christ is in each member of the body, and whether or not they are functioning, according to Christ the Head of the church. It is sad to say, but much of what happens in the body is without the Head. The business of the body is being at the disposal of the Head. If we are the recipients of life, then we will engage in His missional purpose. Parasitic members of the local church can only cling to the organism, but do not have the life of Christ in them. Judas Iscariot was a parasite who did not have the life of Christ flowing through him. However, every authentic member of the body is vital to the growth and vitality of the organism. In body life, the Holy Spirit, as the heart, circulates the life blood through every part of the body. Indeed, this is the glorious church. What a phenomenal truth—I am a member of the second body of Christ in an indispensable union with Christ and one another.

The church, the body of Christ, is glorious as an organism more than an organization. There is a need for order in the church, but in context of the organism life of the body of Christ. Christ, who is Lord of the church and Head of the church, makes order and organization necessary. Christ, as Chief Cornerstone, suggests order—as Peter wrote, *"living stones"* placed in order in the edifice. There is order in the organism.

However, the organism will function merely as an organization without the work and ministry of the Holy Spirit. Why are some members of the organism complacent and inactive when they have been so graciously born and baptized into it? We have discussed being born of the Spirit, the baptism of the Spirit, the indwelling of the Spirit, the gift and gifting of the Spirit, but now we must address the filling of the Spirit.

> *"Do not get drunk with wine, for that is debauchery, but be filled with the Spirit, addressing one another in psalms and hymns and spiritual songs, singing and making melody to the Lord with*

your heart, giving thanks always and for everything to God the Father in the name of our Lord Jesus Christ, submitting to one another out of reverence for Christ" (Ephesians 5:18-21, ESV).

In all of the works and ministries of the Holy Spirit, we notice the indicative, but here we see the imperative in continuum. The passive voice is in play here suggesting the believer's obedient yielding to the Spirit's control. It is dynamic and not stagnant. The wind fills the sail of the ship and moves it along to its destination and purpose. The Spirit, as the Wind, moves members of the body along towards their purpose and destination. This continuum of the Spirit's control is daily walking in the Spirit and being guided by the Spirit.

The advent of the Spirit has taken place. His new place of operations is in every member of the body of Christ. He is resident, at home in every member of the body. The Holy Spirit, who is God, and, therefore, omnipresent, has condescended to live exclusively in each member of the body of Christ. This renders the church as glorious. The church is only glorious when she operates as an organism. And she is only an organism when the Spirit is operative in the body. When there is drifting from operating as an organism to operating merely as an organization, the church is not experiencing body life. When the Spirit is operative in the body, there is music, not for entertainment, but for the enhancement of oneness. And praise to the one God and Father of the Lord Jesus Christ. When the Spirit is operative in worship, there are spiritual songs of testimonial nature, reminding us of the Gospel of grace, wherein the hearts are touched. Moreover, the Spirit is not only operative in worship, but also in the work.

When the church functions as an organism, the Spirit is operative, and body life and purpose is experienced. I have noticed how biblical scholarship and Christian and church familiarity can make us less dependent on the Spirit. We have learned to be Christians so much, that we do not think we need the Spirit. Francis Chan thinks that the Holy

Spirit has become the *Forgotten God* (the title of his book) and purposed to reverse our tragic neglect of the Holy Spirit. He troubles us by saying, "From his perspective, the Holy Spirit is tragically neglected and, for all practical purposes, forgotten. While no evangelical would deny His existence, I'm willing to bet there are millions of churchgoers cross America who cannot confidently say they have experienced His presence or action in their lives over the past year. And many of them do not believe they can."[22] John the Baptist's disciples were unacquainted with the Holy Spirit (Acts 19:2), but, tragically, those who have been born and baptized of the Spirit, operate as if there is no Holy Spirit. How sad. We have the performance enhancing Spirit within us and He is inoperative in our lives. He is number three, the best player, sitting on the bench and we are losing the game of life because we won't call Him into the game. The Holy Spirit is being treated like day workers in our neighborhood waiting to be hired. We need not take Him home with us, He is already resident in us, but inoperative and neglected. Therefore, the best the church can be is an organization, and not an organism. The power of the church is in the presence, purpose, and power of the Spirit who is power. He does not **have** power, He *is* power. The glorious church is the church that operates in the power of the Spirit (Zechariah 4:6). The Spirit in the Old Testament was non-residential, but now He is permanent residential power. Where is the glorious church? It is everywhere that the church is operating as an organism with living stones and the radiant presence of Christ in a dark and benighted world. When the church functions as an organism, it gets into trouble, godly trouble (Acts 17:1-9). Organizational life can make the church of the world, but not so with organism life.

To live as an organism, as members thereof, the crucified life is necessary (Galatians 2:20). It is a past reality with continuous results in the present. It is demonstrated in the prayer life of dependency. It is remaining as children depended on the Father. Never growing out of need for the Spirit of God. As we grow in grace knowledge (2 Peter 3:18), we stay fully aware of our unworthiness and weakness. We must never just grow in knowledge (1 Corinthians 8:1; 2 Corinthians 12:1-10). To be Spirit-filled is to be self-crucified. We must give the control of our lives to the control of the Spirit. Christ cannot live in us effectively until the Spirit controls us effectually. The passive voice in the main text (Ephesians 5:18) denotes our participation in the work of the Spirit. Philippians 2:12-13 reminds us of our need for the Spirit to help us to will and to do God's bidding.

The mystery of the church is that she is a living organism. Christ, the Head of the church, is the resurrected Lord of the church. He is not the historical head of the church, nor is He a dead founder of a movement, but He is the living Head. He is the contemporary of His living church. The church is the redeemed and resurrected community. She exists because of the miracle of the resurrection, and Christ is the resurrection and the life of the church (John 11:25). Each member of this living organism has experienced the Resurrection (Romans 6:4). As Jesus Christ has a glorious, resurrected body, His second body, the church is His glorious, resurrected body on earth (John 17:1, 4, 5, 10, 22, 24). We, as His second body, share the glory of Christ. This glory is primarily manifested in oneness in the body of Christ. Ray Stedman made a tremendous observation: "The calling of the church is to reveal in the world the glory of God's character which is found in the face of Jesus Christ."[23]

The Holy Spirit is the Operation Officer in the church. His advent into the world is a matter of specificity. His omnipresence strongly suggests that His advent into the world is exclusively, effectually present in the believer (John 14:15-17). The mystery of the power within the members of the body is the Holy Spirit. The church is not simply given power but has the powerful person. He is the performance enhancing power within the ordinary, enabling them to function extraordinarily. To function effectively in the body of Christ as witnesses in the world is totally and completely dependent upon the presence and power of the Holy Spirit operating in each member of the organism. In these days of the church, the tragic reality is that the Holy Spirit is inoperative (Ephesians 4:30) and found weeping. The Spirit appears to be operative in worship, but not in the missional purpose of the church. Where is the Holy Spirit these days? He appears to be absent. What a tragic proposition! Can there be church without the Holy Spirit? Is the Holy Spirit spending more time weeping than working His will through us for the glory of God and the edification of the saints?

Chapter 5

The Business

"It is the unfinished business of Christ."

"In the first book, O Theophilus, I have dealt with all that Jesus began to do and teach, until the day when he was taken up, after he had given commands through the Holy Spirit to the apostles whom he had chosen."—Acts 1:1-2, ESV

What is our business? What is the church supposed to be about in the world? What is her contribution in the world? Why is the church here? For whom does she exist? The world has no clue, and many in the visible church are confused concerning what is the business of the church. When those who pastor churches are conflicted about the purposeful presence of the church, what chance do members have in understanding the "why" and the "what" of the church? Jesus' purpose on earth was also misconstrued. His own disciples misunderstood His presence and purpose in the world. They did not look upward, but outward. They did not look inward but outward. His disciples wanted the Davidic kingdom restored (Acts 1:6) and the power and prominence of Israel regained, and Roman dominion defeated, and apartheid removed. They were focused on this world. As Jesus stood before Pilate, who was a puppet authority of Rome and a Jewish sellout, He announced, *"My kingdom is not of this world, if my kingdom were of this world, my servants would have been fighting, that I might not be delivered over to the Jews. But my kingdom is not from the world"* (John 18:36, ESV). Jesus went on to say that His mission in the world was to witness to the truth of which He was the personification of truth (John 14:6). He was the Truth—the truth about God and the truth about man. Through the Incarnation, Jesus as man, becomes the authentic Witness of God. He is the self-disclosure of God. The revelatory presence of God. C. Norman Kraus makes this theological observation: "In Jesus, God shares our life. In the incarnation God shares his life with us."[24]

Jesus, the Authentic Witness, demands that the business of the church be our witness of Him. The unfinished business of the body and her members is to be the ontological presence of Christ. The primary purpose of the body of Christ and those within the body is presence, and then proclamation. The advent of the Spirit into the life of the body is for the purpose of enabling us to tell the truth about Jesus Christ, who is *the* Truth. The work of the Holy Spirit within us is to empower our witness of the Witness.

> *"You will receive power when the Holy Spirit has come upon you, and you will be my witnesses in Jerusalem and in all Judea and Samaria, and to the end of the earth"* (Acts 1:8, ESV).

Yes! We will need the power of the Spirit of truth to be the witness of the truth about Jesus Christ who is the Truth about God and man (John 16:13-15). The revelatory purpose of Jesus must come first. We must see and understand that Immanuel was God with us (Matthew 1:22-23) in order for us to understand that the church, as the body of Christ, is Christ within the world through us. The business of the church is a miraculous mystery. The witness and the work of Jesus are somewhat related, but the witness comes first and is primary.

Jesus, in His earthly ministry, came preaching, teaching and healing (Matthew 4:23-25; 9:35-38). In declaring the gospel of the kingdom, He was not being political or announcing His rule on earth, but His rule within the heart of believers. At this epoch of time, His kingdom would be internal and not external, invisible and not visible and other worldly and not worldly (John 18:33-38). Jesus had no political agenda, although His disciples would have wished He had one (Acts 1:6-7). However, what He wanted them to engage in was being a witnessing community (Acts 1:8) that would reach the world with the gospel of the kingdom—the kingdom in them and them in the kingdom. If Jesus could reign in the heart of men as King, it would affect the human situation. Changing policies would not matter as much if hearts were comprehensively changed. Jesus' healing ministries was somewhat selective, some He did not heal. He did come healing, but His purpose was to authenticate His identity as God, before He would identify Himself as the man of sorrow—kinsman redeemer (Matthew 1:21). The question is asked, if not thought, is Jesus concerned about the social plight of humanity? The answer is yes! "For He will save his people from their sins." All social ills are a matter of sin. Here again, all social conditions are heart problems, rooted in sin. Certainly, they must be confronted by the church, the community of the reconciled, but with the understanding that sin is at the root of all ugliness. Sense all members of humanity, saved and unsaved, sin as a way of life or as a contradiction of the new life, social ills are not skin problems but sin problems.

Signs and wonders marked the ministry of Jesus and the ministry of the apostles and prophets. As the church grew, we see less and less of signs and wonders. We must look at signs and wonders in light of their purpose and not their presence. When viewing their purpose, do we see a need for their presence today? In the following passages, I believe the purpose of signs and wonders are stated (see Acts 2:22; 5:12; 14:3; Hebrews 2:4). They were done primarily by the apostles as witness to their authority and message. This note of caution must be made. Miracles of God are still happening. The unexplainable is still happening in our world, wherein only God is the explanation. My purpose in this paragraph is that I believe the lessening of signs and wonders should find their cessations in the believer becoming the sign and the wonder (Ephesians 2:10). Why are some people so bent on seeing signs rather than being signs and wonders?

What patient would go to a hospital that majored in its cafeteria and gift shop and not patient care? A hospital where the doctors spend the day cooking in the kitchen, nurses spend their time as waitress and the orderly is busy busting tables and washing dishes. Who would send their love ones to a hospital where the surgeons spend more time in the gift shop than the operating room? This is the state of the church when she majors in minors, and minors in majors. If the church is to be effective, she must know why she exists and prioritize its purpose. There is nothing wrong with minors. They just do not need to be majored in. There is much discussion about the purposeful meaning of Luke 4:18. It is often used in a social context to demonstrate Jesus' social ministry. Its reference is found in Isaiah 61:1-2, which has reference to the Messiah who was to come. However, Jesus was declaring that He was the fulfillment of prophesy. Freedom would be found through His ministry, for He is the consummation of the Year of Jubilee that related to economic justice. In His announcement, Jesus transcended it to a spiritual level. If it was merely economics and politics, we must discover the evidence of its fulfilment through His ministry. We must also ask, who would be the object of the Year of Jubilee, all peoples of the world in need of release? Jesus was saying that those who heard Him that day would not be the recipients of the good news of rest. Only the needy and the poor in spirit (Matthew 5:3) would experience spiritual liberty that will impact social freedoms. Minors are necessary, but they are not to become majors. Jesus was more concerned about man's spiritual conditions than man social conditions. For social problems are rooted in the spiritual.

Jesus' preaching, teaching, and healing ministries were minors, in that, His ultimate purpose was to redeem and reconcile the world to Himself through His atoning sacrifice on the cross (Luke 19:10). He was the preacher, the teacher, and the healer, but more so, He was the Savior. Jesus did not experience much opposition in His preaching, teaching, and healing ministries, but His friends and foes attempted to thwart His journey to the cross. Make no mistake, the cross was not Satan's plan. The Jews wanted Jesus dead and so did the devil, but Satan did not want Him to die on the cross. Satan knew that the cross of Christ was a pivotal, life changing place for fallen humanity. It would be a devastating place for him, for his most effective weapon is the notion of death, but it would be defeated at the cross (see Hebrews 2:14-15; Revelation 20:11-15). At the cross, Jesus conquered death (1 Corinthians 15:51-55). In His death, death itself died (see Psalm 49:15; Isaiah 25:8). Before the Resurrection, death was defeated, because Jesus received the stinger; and sin, which pays off in death, is paid in full by the blood of Jesus (Romans 8:37-39). Now, what makes sin, sin is the holiness and righteousness of God, expressed through the law. Therefore, sin is opposite of who God is in His moral nature. Satan did not want to experience this defeat, so, when Jesus was two years old, Satan attempted to destroy Him. At Jesus' temptation in the wilderness, Satan tried to disqualify Him. After Peter had made the great confession, he sought to discourage Jesus while being influenced by Satan. And when Jesus was hanging on the cross, some derided Him and others dissuaded Him by shouting, *"If you are the Son of God, come down from the cross"* (Matthew 27:39-40, ESV). So, Satan was more concerned about Christ's major work on the cross and resurrection than his ancillary ministries. Jesus was a powerful preacher, teacher, and miracle worker (see John 3:2; Mark 1:22; Matthew 7:29).

Be assured, the unfinished business of Christ that the church is called to continue and complete until the end of the church age, is what Jesus majored in doing—reconciling the world (2 Corinthians 5:18-21). All other ministries and concerns of the church must find its end in the ministry and word of reconciliation. As God was working through and in Christ, reconciling the world to Himself, Christ through the Spirit is working through His second body, reconciling the world to God. The church of Jesus Christ is to become the reconciling community of the new humanity among the old humanity, no longer of the old, but in the midst of the old, to influence through, being music and then lyrics, demonstration and proclamation, hope in a hopeless world (2 Corinthians 5:17).

This is the same as majoring in fulfilling the mandate found in the Great Commission:

> *"Then the eleven disciples went away into Galilee, to the mountain which Jesus had appointed for them. When they saw Him, they worshipped Him; but some doubted. And Jesus came and spoke to them, saying, 'All authority has been given to Me in heaven and on earth, go therefore and make disciples of all the nations, baptizing them in the name of the Father and of the Son and of the Holy Spirit, teaching them to observe all things that I have commanded you; and lo, I am with you always, even to the end of the age.' Amen"* (Matthew 28:16-20, NKJV).

Before Jesus left the world, after His primary purpose was finished (John 19:28-30), He authorized those who would become charter members of His second body to reach the entire world—His vision by means of making disciples, His strategy. I speak in depth about the primacy of making disciples in my book *Discipleship according to Jesus*. The working definition of discipleship is found in how Jesus was a discipler to disciples; therefore "a disciple is an obedient follower of Jesus, relating, reflecting, and reproducing disciples."[25] Making disciples is the major business of the church. It is part and partial to the ministry of reconciliation. Evangelism, which is also the major business of the church, is implied in making disciples when we understand in the working definition given above that in the relating and the reflecting is evangelism. As the second body and her members go into the world relating and reflecting, they influence the world through being good news in a bad news world and hope in a hopeless world. As they relate and reflect who Christ is, they do so as video and then audio. The evangelism is first and foremost ontological. Jesus, in Acts 1:8, talks about "you shall be witnesses." In the Great Commission, evangelism is certainly implied, but not stated as the strategy for accomplishing Jesus' vision for His body, the church. It is important to say here that the church of Jesus Christ must be driven by Jesus' vision and strategy for reaching the world with the ministry and word of reconciliation. The major focus of the church must not be Matthew 25:35-40, but Matthew 28:16-20.

There are some challenges when referring to Matthew 25:35-40 that must be addressed to properly refer to it as the business of the church. It is certainly Christians in attitude and action. However, we must ask questions of the passage to understand its importance into the purpose of the body of Christ. The "when," the "what," the "who," the "where," and the "wherefore" must be asked of the pastor. Is this situation presently happening at that time, or is it future in time? What was the condition that warranted a loving response? Just who were the least of brothers? Wherefore, how should we apply this in today's world in reference to the business of the church?

It appears this refers to the future, taking place during the Tribulation period, approaching the millennium. Those saved in the Tribulation, both Jews and Gentiles, are experiencing a refugee's persecution: poverty, imprisonment, hunger, and ill health were desperately in need a Christian response. This was Christians looking out for fellow Christians who were less fortunate. We have an example in Acts 20:1-5 where the saints in Jerusalem were suffering and the Gentiles came to their rescue (see Romans 15:26; Galatians 2:1-10; Corinthians 16:1-4; 2 Corinthians 8:1-7). We must not think the poor and marginalized are automatically members of the family of God (Galatians 6:10). God is on the side of those who are on His side; those whose faith is in Jesus Christ. Is He concerned about sufferings in the world? Yes! But sufferings are a matter of sin in the world. Therefore, Christ's agenda was not to knock away spider webs, but to kill the spider. The church is sent into the world to affect it for good and to share Christian love and benevolence to all men but are not to major in the minors and certainly not minor in majors. We must understand that "man must not live by bread alone" (Matthew 4:4). Bread, but not alone. Social concerns, but spiritual transformation. We must be driven by this reality: *"For what will it profit a man if he gains the whole world and forfeits his soul? Or what shall a man give in return for his soul?"* (Matthew 16:26, ESV). When we major in minors, we may be placing souls in danger of loss. I am concerned that there are those inside the local church who are focused on "bread only." This would suggest that Christianity has become one of the religious constructs in the world. No longer otherworldly in its purpose. Just another doer of good works. Reducing the church of Christ to the level of humanitarianism. We must not be surprised that the worldview of the church is that the church exists in the world for the social welfare of suffering people in the world. The world thought the same thing about Christ: *"He was in the world, and the world was made through him, yet the world did not know him"* (John 1:10, ESV). They did not know who He was nor what He was sent into the world to do. The world must not be allowed to define our purpose. We must not conform to the world but be transformed by a missional purpose that comes from the Lord Jesus Himself (see Matthew 5: 13-16; 28:19-20).

Jesus entered the world with a divine focus (John 5:30). He came to do the will of the Father and not the will of men. He was incarnate in order to substitute Himself for sinful humanity (Hebrews 10:1-7; 2 Corinthians 5:21). Jesus was focused from pre-incarnation at being our vicarious sufferer (1 Timothy 1:15; Luke 9:52). Jerusalem was His destiny, not Capernaum. The activities at Capernaum were mere pit stops. Jesus was mono-focused so must His church be. Bi-focused, tri-focused and multi-focused is the strategy of the enemy to engage us in good things to divert the church from the best thing, the major business of the church. Paul the apostle was also focused (1 Corinthians 2:2). His life was centered on

Christ (Philippians 1:13-30) and the gospel ministry he was born to do. The Great Commission must become our mono-focused insatiable desire to fulfill through the body of Christ. Again, the last thing Jesus said in His valedictorian address, before He graduated from the earth, must not become the least thing we do. The Great Commission cannot become the "Great Omission" according to Dallas Willard.

We must answer for our effectiveness as the body of Christ in our world, "When is the church at her best?" Some have answered, "At her birth." While this may have some validity, it renders the church a thing of the past, and suggest that the church is outmoded and obsolete, historic and thus, not an organism. It says that the church at its birth, had some birth defects or retardation. There has been growth, incarnationally wherein the church has grown up unto the Head of the church. But allow me to answer the query, "When is the church at her best?" From the historical book of Acts.

"Now Saul was consenting to his death. At that time a great persecution arose against the church which was at Jerusalem; and they were all scattered throughout the regions of Judea and Samaria, except the apostles. And devout men carried Stephen to his burial and made great lamentation over him. As for Saul, he made havoc of the church, entering every house, and dragging off men and women, committing them to prison. Therefore, those who were scattered went everywhere preaching the word" (Acts 8:1-4, NKJV).

There are several things in this passage that suggest the church was at her best. It seems that the church thrives in persecution. God allows the negative to move the church to positive action and ministry. Secondly, the church that was to be missional became stagnant and stationary, scattered due to persecution. The church like a pandemic started to spread throughout the known world. She moved from "come ye" to "go ye." The church was disobeying the Great Commission to go into the world and make disciples. They had become comfortable in Jerusalem, but God stirred the nest through persecution, and they became the diaspora.

Thus, the church is at Her best when she scatters. The apostles stayed in Jerusalem, but the church of the laity went. They left the protocol and the regalia of the temple, and the laity became more than spectators. The church is at her best when the church goes beyond the temple and the laity becomes full participants in the ministry of evangelism. The church is at her best when she preaches. Preaching is the business of the entire church. The word *preach* here in this text is evangelize, not kerygma. All those who scattered left Jerusalem preaching—telling their story of salvation about Jesus' story of salvation in the power of the Spirit (Acts 1:8). The church is at her best when she preaches beyond the ordained and licensed preachers. Much of the preaching will be music, and then with lyrics, demonstration, and then proclamation.

Prior to the birth of the church is the pre-identification of the church as salt and light. Matthew 5:13-16 describes also the ontological business of the church. Ontological, yes! Because salt and light just "be." These business metaphors are silent, but substantive. The emphatic pronoun, "you are the salt," and "you are the light" are the properties of the church alone. No one else possesses these designations. This is the sole business of the church. Without the church in the world, the world is void of these properties. The world stands salt-less and dark. The church, as community, becomes the righteousness of God in the world holding back moral corruption. As salt, the church's business is to make the world thirsty for God, to preserve, and bring flavor to the flavorless world. Also, as salt, the church fertilizes the world preparing a way to the Lord. And the church as community are lights shining forth truth in darkness. Lights are visible witnesses of the truth about Jesus Christ (Acts 1:8). Not hidden like but on a light stand as a city on the hill shining in darkness, shining the way to Jesus who saves. Again, the church's light is reflective in nature, the lesser light, while Jesus is the greater light. The revelation of God. The Truth about God. The Witness and the Amen of God. Christ is the Sun we are the moon. This is a glorifying purpose; the world sees God's workmanship in us (Ephesian 2:10; Matthew 5:16).

I am writing this work at a time when there is great division within the church—a division that I have not experienced in my lifetime. However, division is not new to the church. The division is affecting our witness and viability in the world. We are to be influential in the world as salt and light, but the division in the church thwarts our influence. There are divisions between the Black and White churches, and there are divisions within the black church itself. The divisions between the black and white churches are more sociological, and the divisions within the Black churches is more theological. While the enemy, fundamentally is Satan, we can function as agents of Satan in perpetuating the division. In Scripture and church history, to deal with divisions in the church, councils were formed: the Jerusalem council (Acts 15); the Council of Nicaea (AD 325); Council of Constantinople (AD 381); Council of Ephesus (AD 431); Council of Chalcedon (AD 451), and so on, to solve problems of doctrinal division, that threatened the life and health of the church. I think, it is time for church councils to be formed around Scripture and prayer. Our witness in the world as the body of Christ is being *"weighed on the scales and found wanting."*

There is a frightening situation found in 1 Corinthians 3:1-11. There were two groups of people who disrespected the unity by causing division in the local congregation, a microcosm of the body of Christ. They were church members, who were also members of the body of Christ, who were old infants creating a party system within the church. There were also church members, who are non-members of the body of Christ, causing division for the purpose of destroying the church's witness in the world through false teaching (see Acts 20:29-30; Jude 1:4). God will destroy the latter group and their works (1 Corinthians 3:17). But the old infants, the church members who belong to the body of Christ, will suffer loss in the area of rewards (1 Corinthians 3:15). I offer this passage for us to think seriously about being a part of division in the church. We must fight to maintain the unity of the church. Where is the fight in us to maintain the practical oneness that is true of us positionally?

The business of the church, the body of Christ, is to represent Christ in the world from the other world. *"Now then, we are ambassadors for Christ, as though God were pleading through us: we implore you on Christ's behalf, be reconciled to God"* (2 Corinthians 5:20, NKJV). We have come from the world. We once were of the world. We were darkness (see Ephesians 5:8-14; 1 Peter 2:9). But we have been delivered and translated into the kingdom of the Son (Colossians 1:13). We are no longer indigenous to this world, but strangers and aliens (1 Peter 2:11) sent back into the world to represent and speak for Christ as His ambassadors. Truly we are in the world but not of the world (John 17:16-26). The ontological business of the body of Christ through the visible church is to be different. The church cannot make a difference until it is different. First Corinthians 5:17 is the essence of that difference: *"Therefore, if anyone is in Christ, he is a new creation. The old has passed away; behold, the new has come"* (2 Corinthians 5:17, ESV). We are different because of the miracle that Christ has wrought in us. We are a new humanity, new in kind and not in time. Thus, we have a new worldview, a new perspective from the kingdom of heaven. The old man has become the new man. Therefore, we are driven not by old business but the new business of the kingdom of God. The church is not the kingdom, but the colony of the kingdom. Jesus taught His disciples to pray, *"Your kingdom come, your will be done, on earth as it is in heaven"* (Matthew 6:10, ESV).

The ambassador's business of the church, the colony of the kingdom, is to represent and speak the will of God in the world. The will of God being done in the members of the body of Christ by living transformed and transparent lives. Here again is the idea of being video, visible witnesses as ambassadors. Audio is very important, being spokesman of the kingdom is necessary. The speaking business of the kingdom will come as we speak truth to power as Jesus did. But the power of our words, as we represent Christ, will come through our behavior. I cannot stress this enough; the transformed and transparent life is pivotal to making a difference in this foreign land. We must expose to the world, otherworldliness, answering the query: "What would I have if I had Jesus?" The church must answer this question not with proclamation as much as demonstration. I don't think that the world is looking for a sermon but the advantage of the Christian life. How will giving my life to Jesus benefit me in the now, and not in the by and by? How will Jesus Christ affect my relationship, marriage and family, parenting, economics, my longings, fears, anxieties, hopelessness, failures, inward struggles, and more? They want your life to be an example of what it is like to have Christ at work in one's life. All of this calls for transparency. As ambassadors for Christ, we represent Christ and His kingdom in person and not merely in the principles of kingdom. As ambassadors, we are profiles of the kingdom of God found in the Beatitudes in Matthew 5:3-12. As ambassadors, we are living the kingdom life in the church age.

The ambassador became the seasoned saint through the process that began at the new birth (John 3:3-8) by recognizing he is poor in spirit. This designation celebrates spiritual poverty. Happy is the man who realizes he needs a Savior for he is lost. He is not deceived by his riches, righteousness, or religiousness. He is aware of his insufficiency. He knows he is spiritually bankrupt, and the debt is far greater than he is able to pay. The rich in spirit are Pharisees who don't need a physician, thus, far from the kingdom. The kingdom will never be accessible to them (Luke 18:9-29). In the parable of the Pharisee and the publican, we see the poor in spirit in the cry for mercy while the rich in spirit congratulated himself in his supposed worthiness. Jesus teaches that the kingdom belongs only to the poor in spirit who come like a child to Him. He continues to describe the poor in spirit as those who would surrender all to enter the kingdom. There is no boasting in those who are poor in spirit. Those who are rich in spirit will never enter the kingdom and they will never have the kingdom in them. Sensing your poverty in spirit is necessary to becoming a citizen of the kingdom of God. The consciousness of helplessness and hopelessness leads to becoming a citizen of the kingdom of heaven. We must preach the Gospel that causes the hearer to sense his or her utter need for salvation through Christ alone, through grace alone, and through faith alone. It is impossible with man to please God, gaining favor with Him apart from Him. We are totally unmerited, depraved in spiritual death. If God does not act, we cannot have life eternal. The hindrances to entering the kingdom of God and becoming citizens are an improper sense of self-esteem, humanism, pride, self-worth, self-righteousness, self-sufficiency, religiosity, and morality. Therefore, blessed are the beggars for the kingdom belongs to them.

The ambassador is a citizen of the kingdom of which the church is a colony. He is identified as the mournful. Blessed are the sad. How strange. He who is mournful or sad is to be congratulated. This seems antithetical to happy. Congratulations for sadness seems contradictory. Why? Because they will be comforted and strengthened together. Because they see sin as God sees it and they mourn. They are saddened because of the effects of sin—death (see Ezekiel 18:20; Romans 6:23). Sin does lead to sadness and death, but this is not sadness after the fact, rather before the sin of action. It is a beatitude. A way of thinking and behaving opposite of the world. It is kingdom thinking and behaving. It is possessing God's attitude towards sin, causing the pursuit towards righteousness and holiness. It leads to seeking God's will more than God's forgiveness. The mournful will seek the will of God so that they will not always have to seek His forgiveness. The mournful are blessed and congratulated for it is evidence of having the nature of God (1 John 3:9-10).

Who are the mournful? In pertaining to sin, the mournful are those who reside in a state of hatred toward sin. They perpetually remain in sackcloth and ashes. They live in opposition to sin. They are marked out by their constant struggles with sin. There is always this tension between the flesh and the Spirit (Galatians 5:16-17) that is ongoing in the life of the mournful. This fight with sin is ongoing, although the power of sin has been broken (Romans 6:1-23). We are no longer slaves to sin, no longer under the reign and dominion of sin. The mournful have said yes to the Lord and no to Satan. This is repentance. If there is no mournfulness in the saint over sin, there is probably mutuality with Satan and the flesh. If you are in common, comfortable, and complicit with sin and Satan, you are not blessed. The mournful are uncomfortable and contrite when it comes to sin (Psalm 5:1-19). The mournful realizes that sin is against the who-ness and the what-ness of God. In sin, we lie against the moral nature of God. Sin is adulterous in nature (see Matthew 12:39; Hosea 4:1-19). If there is no sadness concerning sin, there is sameness with Satan.

The mournful are sin fighters. They are against all forms of sin in the world. They view sin as anti-God, anti-man, and anti-cosmos. The mournful hate sin like God hates it. God sent His Son into the world to undo what sin had done against God, against man, and against creation. The mournful confront sin personally in his or her private lives and, if not, it will disqualify the public life of the ambassador.

The ambassador is sent into the world as the meek. He has entered the kingdom through the new birth by means of brokenness. The kingdom men and women are tamed by the power of the Gospel of grace. Gentleness and meekness are actually strength under control. The wild stallion is tamed to do the will of the rider. The meek are those who have surrendered to the will of the Master. They live under authority of the King, the Lord of the kingdom. In sin, they were in rebellion to the will and purpose of God (Isaiah 53:6). As the sinner enters the kingdom through the new birth he or she enters bowed down to the will of the King. The intellect, the emotions, and the will are matter of faith meeting grace. The will of man is changed to "thy will be done, not mine." Here is where the Lordship of Jesus Christ begins, the surrendered will to the will of the Lord. Lordship is found in the will element of faith. The proud Pharisee, Nicodemus or Saul of Tarsus will not enter the kingdom standing up but bowing down to Jesus of Nazareth. Jesus is Lord of lord and King of kings. Ambassadors become so, because they have entered the kingdom on their knees of submission to the will of the Lord.

We are no earthly good in the business of the kingdom when approaching the world in arrogance and pride. Jesus came to the earth in meekness, in His humanity and humiliation. Our salvation and citizenship in the kingdom are a matter of His weakness and not His strength (2 Corinthians 13:4; Philippians 2:5-10). It was not Jesus the Lion of Judah, but Jesus the Lamb of Calvary, who became weak that we might be saved.

The ambassadors of the kingdom of God have an insatiable hunger and thirst for righteousness. Those in the kingdom have an appetite for God's standards found in God's written Word. Those in right relationship with the Lord hunger, thirst, and seek for the kingdom rule and the righteous principles of the kingdom (Matthew 6:33). They long for God's Word, not merely for head knowledge, but for heart conformity to the will of God. It is transformation. The seeker of righteousness desires to become more like Him (see Romans 8:29; Galatians 4:19; 1 Peter 2:1-3, 2 Peter 3:18). If you are living an unsatisfied, incomplete life as a Christian, check your eating habits and diet. Do you have an appetite for the Word of God which comes from being born-again through the living and enduring Word of God (1 Peter 1:23)? Those in the kingdom have become "slaves of righteousness" with an insatiable desire for righteousness. They are starving for righteousness (Romans 6:15-23). The ambassadors of the kingdom practice righteousness because of their position of righteousness (1 John 2:29; 3:7-10).

The ambassadors are authentic representatives. They are pure in heart, unmixed in motive and purpose. Like John the Baptist, they are the voices of the King of the kingdom. Speaking the King's words is their pure purpose. Their motives are to speak the King's message of reconciliation in this foreign land. They are from another country and speak the

King's words in this foreign country. Although their loyalty is to another country, they are patriots of the kingdom of God, and they vigorously support the agenda of the kingdom of heaven, prepared to defend it against the onslaughts of Satan, the insidious nature of the flesh, and the invasive sinful system of the world, and other detractors of the faith. Ambassadors are not loyal to political parties—donkeys or elephants—but to the Lamb and the Lion, Jesus Christ (see John 1:29; Revelation 5:5-14). The ambassadors of the kingdom are loyal to Jesus Christ, and to Him alone, who is worthy. All other kingdoms will someday bow to the most glorious kingdom of which the church is a colony (see Philippians 2:10-11; Revelation 1:7-8; 11:15).

The business and function of the community of ambassadors is to represent the King in conduct and communication. They are to act like who they are, the reconciled, and then they are to engage in the ministry and word of reconciliation. As ambassadors, we are in right relationship with God through the atoning activity of Christ (Romans 5:1-11). Then we are to tell of it in a world that has gone astray from God (Isaiah 53:6). The message the ambassador brings from the King is that the Lord laid on Jesus Christ "the iniquity of us all" (2 Corinthians 5:21). These are wonderful words from the far country. The pure in heart, the real and authentic witness, is in the business of assisting the blind to see God. It is only when we are pure at the center of our being that sinners can see God through us. Those who are pure in heart, in their transparency, magnify God (Psalm 34:3) and exalt Jesus' name as the body of Christ. Who is the object of seeing God? The pure in heart, the real, and the authentic? Or the people groping in darkness?

The ambassadors are sent back into the world with a new heart, a heart of flesh and not of stone (see Ezekiel 36:26; Hebrews 8:10). It is pure because it has been transformed, renewed by the Holy Spirit (Romans 5:5; 12:1-2). They shall see God because they saw God. They will see Him because they have seen Him. In order to see Him on Mount Calvary in grace (John 1:17; Galatians 3:24-25), they saw Him on Mount

Sinai in the Law. They have seen Him in the beauty of holiness, to see Him in the splendor of grace. At Calvary the ambassadors received their sight. They saw Him in salvation and sanctification and, finally, they will see Him in glorification (1 John 3:1-3). They see God in providence, in persecutions, in pain, in plenty, in poverty and in pleasure.

Seeing God is comprehensive. The ambassador has seen, is seeing, and will see Him. But the world will see God in Christ through the community of ambassadors. They cannot see God without the church transacting business in the world. The church, the second body of Christ, reflects Him in the world. Listen to this marvelous truth concerning Jesus: *"No one has ever seen God; the only God, who is at the Father's side, he has made him known"* (1:18, ESV). The purpose of the ambassadors, as members of the second body of Christ, is to make Him known in the world. And when the assignment is completed, the ambassadors will be summoned home.

> *"As I journey through the land, singing as I go, pointing souls to Calvary to the crimson flow, many arrows pierce my soul from without, within; but my Lord leads me on, through Him I must win.*
>
> *Oh, I want to see Him, look upon His face, there to sing forever of His saving grace; on the streets of glory let me lift my voice, cares all past, home at last, ever to rejoice."*[26]

In this matter of seeing God, it must be understood that we will only see God the Father in the face of Jesus (2 Corinthians 4:1-6). The unseen God is revealed in the Word become flesh (see Matthew 11:27; John 1:18). Ambassadors of Christ are in the business of peacemaking. Ambassadors of Christ have peace with God made possible through Christ. And Christ accomplished it through the death on the cross. Through the Atonement, sinners have gone from enemies to emissaries by the judicial act of God declaring the sinner right with Himself (Romans 5:1, 2). All this is a matter of grace through faith. Undeserved sinners in rebellion are the object of this gracious act of reconciliation. We also have the peace of God that comes from inward contentment. Moreover, we have the character of Jesus Christ, the Prince of Peace, expressed in the Fruit of the Spirit (see Philippians 4:7; Galatians 5:22-23). It is necessary in the ministry of reconciliation to have the Fruit of the Spirit that is innate to the new birth (2 Corinthians 5:19-20). We are on a peace mission in a world that is at odds with God and man in discord with one another. Strife and division inside the church contradict the church's purpose and business as peacemakers as well as our sonship and oneness in the body. Peacemaking is found in the church's presence, not at the negotiating table. Peacemaking is atmospheric. The peacemaker is not necessarily passive nor aggressive, but fruit bearing—a paragon of peace.

Ambassadors in the foreign land experience persecution because of the counter distinctive of the kingdom of God. One would wonder, why do peacemakers experience persecution? You would think they would be welcomed in the world. Well, it is the nature and objectives of peacemaking that leads to persecution. The ambassador's peace making is paradoxical in nature. Like Jesus, the Prince of Peace, peacemakers cause separation in order to bring reconciliation (Matthew 10:34). Jesus was misunderstood and so are the members of the kingdom colony. Peace did come to earth through Jesus Christ, but it was rejected (John 1:11). Peace cannot be experienced on earth when man has marshalled himself against God. When man chooses to abandon God for the religion of humanism, there can be no peace vertically nor horizontally.

It is the nature and ministry of the peacemaker that brings persecution to him (see 2 Timothy 3:12; 1 Peter 4:12-19; John 15:18-21). When the world is pleased with the church, we can be sure God is not (James 4:4). Why are we not blessed? And why are we not persecuted? Why are we not approved of God—blessed? Why are we not receiving a standing ovation from Jesus (Acts 7:56)? When we are persecuted by the world, it is more about how we live than by what we believe. Persecution will be experienced, often subtly, when we are salt of the earth and light in the world. Being godly will beget trouble with the ungodly. Being not of the world will cause you to be hated by the world.

What exactly does "for righteousness' sake" mean? Righteousness is what is deemed as right according to His moral nature. It is His standard for the kingdom, living inside and outside the fellowship of the church. We become aware that it is His righteousness when persecution follows. Remember, the world is antagonistic towards God and the godly. The kingdom of light and the kingdom of darkness are opposites. The ungodly in atheism is more obvious than the ungodliness in democracy. There is an ungodliness inside democracy that is more dangerous than communism. The world is being the world, but is the church being the church? The church is being the church where there is persecution. Most religious constructs claim persecution as a mark of authenticity. But we speak of suffering for Jesus' name sake, and righteousness sake. Persecution is not to be sought; it is automatic through obedience to the Word of God. If you are not experiencing persecution on some level, overt or covert, you are probably not pursuing holiness and righteousness. You are to be congratulated when persecuted, for it identifies your kinship with the Lord Jesus and His prophets of old. We rejoice not *in* sufferings but in the opportunity to bring glory to God *through* sufferings.

The business of the church is best driven by mercy and grace. Jesus said, *"Blessed are the merciful, for they shall receive mercy"* (Matthew 5:7, ESV). When the body of Christ remembers that they were "poor in spirit," they will live with mercy towards others in the church and outside the church. Those who have experienced mercy in salvation are merciful (Ephesians 2:4-7). Kingdom citizens extend mercy to those who do not deserve it. Because we have received God's mercy, we extend some slack to others inside and outside the kingdom. The poor in spirit are ungrateful servants when they are not merciful. Another way to express it is those who have received grace and are driven by it are merciful. The more we grow in grace knowledge, the more merciful we become (2 Peter 3:18). Mercy is longsuffering while grace is God in Christ suffering in our stead. Mercy is God's patience with us, but grace is Christ, our propitiation (see 2 Peter 3:9; 1 John 2:2). Now grace goes further than mercy. Mercy has an expiration date, while grace is timeless, unlimited and boundless. The unmerciful prove that they have not received mercy or have become ungrateful servants.

Jesus performed acts of mercy on His way to demonstrate grace on Calvary. His main purpose was to purchase our redemption. But on His way to Calvary, He expressed mercies in places like Capernaum. The miracles He did were His mercies extended. Jesus was the miracle worker, but it was not the main reason He came to earth. Through miracles of Jesus, we see rivers of mercy flowing into the ocean of grace. Jesus was mercy in the flesh, the personification of compassionate mercy. Most of His acts of mercy led to His ultimate mission on earth (John 12:9-11). His acts of mercy were springboards to fulfilling His redemptive purpose (Luke 19:10). Both mercy and grace find definition in the holiness and righteousness of God. Mercy and grace are not needed, if there is no wrong, no sin, no offense, or no hurt. In mercy, you go out of your way to perform kindness towards others (Luke 10:25-37). As they came from worship, the Priest and the Levite wouldn't even cross the street to be merciful to a man in pain. I ponder whether or not either of them truly experienced God in worship. But the Good Samaritan acted like Jesus, the Great Samaritan, who went out of His way, from heaven to earth, from divinity to humanity, and from Capernaum to Calvary. Jesus became marginalized for those who lived on a marginal level of life. The Good Samaritan gave himself, but the Great Samaritan gave His life a ransom for many. When we are merciful, we are most like Jesus for you are merciful when serving others. We do not receive God's mercy by being merciful (Titus 3:5); rather, we are merciful because we have experienced God's mercy. You express mercy, because you have experience it in Christ

Jesus. Mercy is first a noun, and then a verb (1 Peter 2:9-10). It may seem like mercy is conditional, but it is not. It is unconditional. Our salvation is not a condition on our showing mercy but on being the recipients of mercy. We can extend it because we have received it. Fred Fisher said, "Jesus did not mean we buy the mercy of God by being merciful; it is not a matter of tit for tat. Such a thought would violate the whole spirit of the New Testament and make our salvation a commercial transaction. Rather, our mercy is a sign that we have received mercy. Receiving it fits us to extend mercy."[27] Robert Guelich, stated this way, "In other words, those who will receive mercy are those who now have experienced it and practice it in view of God's work through Jesus Christ."[28] Both of these men are saying that practitioners of mercy are possessors of mercy. We have unconditional mercy, in receiving and in extending it.

Unusual mercy is found in the church, the colony of the kingdom of God. There is mercy shown in the world by unbelievers and in other religious constructs. But kingdom mercy transcends other expressions of mercy—it is God-like. It is vertical and then horizontal. It comes down from God in Christ and then out to man. The Christian is reflecting the mercy of God through the new nature. Mercy is related to forgiveness, wherein you have the power to harm or punish someone due to the wrong done to you, but instead you release them from harm or punishment. You have a right for justice to be done on your behalf, but you forgive. There is unmerited forgiveness in mercy (Matthew 18:21-35). In the Old Testament, the "Mercy Seat" was the place where forgiveness was symbolized. The cross of Calvary was where forgiveness was actualized, and the body of Christ is the place where forgiveness is realized and unusual mercy was demonstrated for the world to see (see Ephesians 4:29-32; Colossians 3:12-13). Unforgiveness is the ungratefulness of grace. In refusing to forgive others, you remove God as preeminent, making yourself the preeminent one (Psalm 51:4). Sin is primarily against God, and secondarily against man. When you don't forgive and God does, you place yourself above Him. Therefore, unforgiveness in the colony of the kingdom is more atrocious than it being practiced in the world. The King forgives, but His servants will not. For the sake of our witness, the church must be the place of mercy. Where is mercy? It is in the character of the citizens of the kingdom (Galatians 5:22-24). The properties of mercy are found in the Fruit of the Spirit. This is who we are before what we do. We have been mercified in order to be merciful—showing mercy.

Where there is no mercy, we will find ourselves under judgment (1 Peter 4:17). The judgment seat of Christ is not in view here, but Christian discipline in the body of Christ. It speaks more of the mistreatment inside the colony of the kingdom. Perhaps this is purifying judgment. The church's trajectory adjusted towards mercy inside and not outside the family of God. This may be a Kairos moment, a crucial time in the life of the church. When the Red Cross is more compassionate than the church, judgment may be at the door of the church. I realize that Matthew 25:31-46 is future in fulfillment, but it must be our practice in the now. However, it does have eternal significance. For where there is no mercy in the verb sense, it may reveal that there is none in the noun sense. Are we the merciful that practice mercy? Do we have the character of God as it pertains to mercy? Selective mercies cannot be in the church, the place of mercy (Galatians 6:10). Members of the body of Christ are the primary place of manifesting mercy, but secondarily we must show mercy elsewhere in the world. The fruit of mercy is no more or less than the Fruit of the Spirit manifested in the power of the Spirit towards others, especially those in the colony of the kingdom. Joseph extended mercy to his brothers who harmed him out of jealousy and sold him as a slave (Genesis 45:1-15). Lastly, mercy is more than forgiveness and forbearance. God's mercies are new every morning through the providential care of God. Mercy is not always related to sin, but because we live in a fallen world because of sin, mercy is God extending time through healing mercies and raining on the just and unjust. Mercy is a matter of life. We exist on the mercies of God. Mercy suits our case in life, and especially in salvation. Showing mercy is the business of the colony of the kingdom as witnesses to God in Christ.

The glorious church is called to do business in the marketplace of life. She is not called to go to church. Although worship and discipleship are essential to the church's health, calling us to gather, Jesus called into being the church to be missional and the diaspora in the world, spreading the Gospel of grace where we live, work, learn and play. We are not to become stationary, but missionary. Not come ye, but "go ye" into your concentric circle of influence and make, mark, mature, and multiply disciples.

Chapter 6

The Blessed

"It is for the sake of the world we exist."

"Therefore, if anyone is in Christ, he is a new creation. The old has passed away; behold, the new has come. All this is from God, who through Christ reconciled us to himself and gave us the ministry of reconciliation; that is, in Christ God was reconciling the world to himself, not counting their trespasses against them, and entrusting to us the message of reconciliation. Therefore, we are ambassadors for Christ, God making his appeal through us. We implore you on behalf of Christ, be reconciled to God."—2 Corinthians 5:17-20, ESV

"As you sent me into the world, so I sent them into the world."—John 17:18, ESV

The nation of Israel was called into existence to be a blessing to the whole world. They would be a channel through which God would bless the entire world. They were His special people for a special purpose. God blessed Israel in spite of their disobedience and wandering astray. God's hand of mercy was surely upon them. The womb of Israel produced Jesus, the Savior of the world, and they were to be a witness as a nation to God's purpose in Jesus the Messiah. The humanity and the humility of Jesus caused many to reject Him as their Messiah (John 1:12). Did they understand their missional purpose? Did the purpose of their existence dead-end in them? The church is not the new Israel, although the church is comprised of both Jew and Gentile forming one new man. This was the mystery hidden but now revealed. The church is not an afterthought. She is as purposed as Christ is purposed in eternity past to show up redemptively in human history. What a tremendous privilege to be associated with the greatest gift ever given to mankind, God's gift of His Son. The golden text of Scripture, which is most glorious, declares, *"For God so loved the world that He gave His only begotten Son that whoever believes in Him should not perish but have everlasting life"* (John 3:16, NKJV). In this gift, God threw in all that He had. He lavished humanity with heaven's best. The gift of His Son was the ultimate extreme expression of His love for sinful humanity. What made it so amazing was that the gift was undeserved in the case of the potential recipients. *"But God shows his love for us in that while we were still sinners, Christ died for us"* (Romans 5:8, ESV).

In Jesus Christ, God offered Himself, as the gift. It is a personal gift. The gift was not merely wrapped in swaddling clothes, but in human flesh (John 1:14). He gave Himself for a ransom for many (Mark 10:45). It was not an impersonal system of philosophical thoughts, but Himself He gave. In creation God gave life, but because sin entered the world through Adam, and death through sin, life was interrupted (Romans 5:12). God moved again and gave His Son to interrupt death with eternal life through His Son (John 5:24). Jesus became the consummate gift. He is the ultimate gift. He became the definitive gift. The Father gave the gift of His Son, and the Son gave the gift of His life that believers may experience the gift of eternal life. Moreover, the Giver keeps giving. He gave the believer the gift of the Holy Spirit (Acts 2:38). Every believer has been endowed with the presence and power of the Spirit (Romans 8:9-11). The Father sends Jesus into the world, but the Father and Son sent the Holy Spirit to indwell believers in the world (see John 14:25, 26; 16:5-11). The sending of the Spirit is in correlation with Christ's sending His church into the world. The advent of the Holy Spirit is a new dimension of the Third Person of the Trinity. He is eternally omnipresent but has selected to exclusively be operative in believers through the body of

Christ on earth. The gift of the Spirit is for the purpose of enabling the gift of the church to exist for the sake of the salvation of the world.

I am surprised that inside the church some are tripping over the devaluation of the church by the unchurched and those who desire a churchless Christianity. Jesus warned His disciples that if they devalue Him, the ultimate gift to the world, that they would also devalue themselves who were pregnant with the church that would be birthed at Pentecost (John 15:18-19). When Jesus came into the world as a gift, primarily to the Jews, they devalued and rejected the gift (John 1:10-11). The church today is often devalued for the same reason Jesus was devalued. The world misunderstands the real reason for the existence of the church in the world. Jesus' own people and disciples initially had the wrong idea for Christ's church. Although the church is a gift to the world, she does not exist to please the world. The church cannot march to the drum beat of the culture, but of Christ, the Head of the church. There will always be a problem with the unchurched and the churchless without an authentic encounter with Christ. It might be that we are too concerned with getting people back in church when they probably left church because they were not members of the body of Christ, only members of the local church. Perhaps, the outsiders—and some insiders—devalue the church because they have not understood or embraced Christ's vision for the church (Matthews 28:19-20).

There is another reason for the devaluation of the church that is much more troublesome. It is the devaluing behavior of members in the body of Christ. Members of the body of Christ devalue the church when it is easy to neglect to assemble together in corporate worship (Hebrews 10:25). When corporate worship appears to be an interruption and worship not a priority, there is devaluation. When worship is merely on your to-do list and not a necessity as an extension of your walk with the Lord, and when work and recreation is more important than corporate worship, there is devaluation. Jesus valued the church to the extent of giving

His life for its existence. Each member has a covenant responsibility to be a functional part of the reincarnation presence of Christ on earth. This existential purpose should humble and cause members to be in awe of the privilege of membership in the organism. We devalue the church when we do not "seek to maintain the unity of the Spirit in the bond of peace" (Ephesians 4:3, 31-32), striving to be peacemakers. Where there is ungrace, there will be devaluation.

The church is devalued when her purpose is not in line with Christ's purpose for His church. The value of the church is measured by whether or not she functions as designed by Christ. Christ values an obedient church; however, the culture values *our* church and not *His* church. His church obeys the Great Commandment and the Great Commission. The value of the church stems from the radicalization of each member's experience in regeneration. There is much concern these days of the radicalization of the Jihadists and Isis. They have disturbed our way of life in America and the world. They have declared war on those whom they view as their enemies. It is not a fight against a nation as much as an ideological fight. They are doing what the church of Jesus Christ should be doing (Acts 17:6)—turning the world upside down. The radical church is called to disturb the sinful system that orders the affairs of the culture. It is called to radicalize sinners, recruiting them for the sake of Christ and His kingdom with the radical Gospel of grace. Yes! Our value is in being different to make a difference in the world and culture. We cannot become State churches, conforming to the culture. We must dare to be countercultural. As Ahab rightly accused Elijah of troubling Israel (1 Kings 18:17-18), the church must trouble the sinful culture and the authorities. We must not become one with the culture, but above the culture (see John 15:18, 19; Romans 12:1-2). The church is called to impact the world, not to impress, and import the world's values. The question must be asked, "What difference is the church making in the world?" The inhabitants of Jericho experienced the miraculous power of God through Israel's victory and became fainthearted because of Israel

(Joshua 2:24). The power of the Resurrection should make the world fainthearted because of us. The effects of Jesus' resurrection should so impact the members of the body of Christ that the church's presence in the world is revolutionary. The resurrection of Jesus Christ is not only a historical fact according to the apostle Paul, but also an existential reality of the Christians experience and the church's expression (Romans 6:1-23). Through the dynamic of the Resurrection, Christians are delivered from the bondage of sin and have become slaves of righteousness.

In our quest to save the church from experiencing decline and death, we cannot let the world define our purpose. The world may view the church as irrelevant and out of step with the culture, but we must please Christ who sent us into the world as a gift to the world for the glory of God. We cannot allow their devaluation and rejection to move us away from Christ's purpose for the church. The church is at her best when she is out of step with the world, but in step with Christ's mission in the world. Albeit authentic members of the body of Christ must not be guilty of devaluing the church by not being good stewards of our membership through the local congregation, a microcosm of the body of Christ. A Christian that is an irresponsible, disconnected, inactive, and an unprincipled member, is a rogue Christian and by their conduct devalues the church. Membership in the body of Christ through the local congregation is a holy stewardship (1 Corinthians 3:16). Solo Christians are just as selfish as those who cause strife and division in the church (1 Corinthians 3:3; 12:12-26). Although we are saved individually, we are saved to do life together. It is not Christ's design for Christians to grow in and through a churchless environment. Worshipping together is important, but doing life together is more important. Focusing on becoming a church with small groups, one-on-one discipleship, with the family being the primary place to make, mark, mature, and multiply disciples is a good strategy for doing life together.

We must reexamine our comprehension and appreciation of the church. Are we truly aware that the church is a gift to the world? I do not expect the world to understand nor to appreciate this fact. But we as members of Christ's body should realize that we are a gift to the world. As Christ is God's Christmas gift to the world, the church is Christ's Pentecostal gift to the world. In what sense is the church Christ's gift to the world? The church is a gift of hope to a hopeless world. There are several passages in Scripture that declare this hope, but, for now, I will concentrate on 2 Corinthians 5:17-21. The church is a gift to the world for we have the message of hope. Just as the Father sent Jesus into the world as a gift, Jesus sends His church into the world as the gift to the world. This truth is captured in the Lord's Prayer—not the model prayer—but the Lord's intercessory prayer for His disciples and us. He prays for us who would be responsible for the continuation of His work in the world. What a glorious privilege given to the church and her members. God, the Father, the eternal God, the sovereign God, the omnipresent God, the omniscient God, the omnipotent God, the immutable God, the Creator God, has preordained that the church of Jesus Christ would be His gift to the world.

As Jesus was the gift, so His church is the gift. He was not a gift to the world; He was the designated and definitive gift to the world. And so is His church. It is a matter of exclusivity and specificity. Christ alone and His church alone is the gift to the world. However, I must not ignore that Jesus was a gift wrapped in the flesh of the nation of Israel before He was wrapped in human flesh. With this in mind, Israel was a gift to the world because He entered the world through the womb of Israel (Genesis 12:1-3; Galatians 4:4). The hope of the world was in the loins of Abraham and His seed (Galatians 3:16). As a nation, Israel rejected and devalued Jesus (John 1:12-13). God's turning to the Gentiles in His salvific focus is not a rejection of Israel, nor is it a refusal to offer salvation to them (Romans 11:11-36). The church is not an afterthought of God, replacing

Israel as God's gift to the world. The church is composed of both Jews and Gentiles. In the nation of Israel were both believers and unbelievers, but the body of Christ is composed of only believers (see Romans 9:6-13; 30-33; 10:1-4). Let me be clear here, in the local congregation there are both believers and unbelievers, but in the body of Christ, there are only believers. The church of Christ is God's plan "A." He has no plan "B." Christ cannot go elsewhere for He is one with His church. He is Head of His body, the church. He is the Bridegroom, and His church is the Bride, and what God has joined together let no man put asunder (Matthew 16:18; 19:6).

As Jesus came preaching, so the church is sent into the world as the preaching community. Like His predecessor, John the Baptist, Jesus came preaching, repent for the kingdom of heaven is here (Matthew 4:17). Please note that John was a gift, for his name denotes this fact. John the Baptist, the Old Testament prophet in the New Testament, was also a gift to the world (John 1:6). He was a forerunner, and the church is an after-runner. In Jesus the kingdom of heaven and its message had come down to earth. A new sphere of existence had invaded the old. Now the apostle Paul reminds the Christians in Corinth that they were a new creation in the midst of the old with a new message. Like Jesus, they *had* a message, and they *were* a message. We will elaborate on this truth later in this book. The kingdom of God or heaven is commensurate in Jesus, and in continuum in the church. Through the kingdom, the King reigns, rules, and reaches out to a sinful world. I will back into this passage (2 Corinthians 5:17-21) and go back and forth to delineate "the church as God's gift to the world."

The world collectively and individually has gone astray from God who is holy. Sin has separated man from God (Isaiah 53:6; 59:2). A divorce has occurred between the Divine and the human. Spiritual adultery led to spiritual dissolution. The state of humanity is spiritual death (Ephesians 2:1-3). If this condition and state of man is not dealt with, the consequence is eternal death. God, the one who has been sinned against, moves towards man, for man is unable to move towards Him. The church pregnant with the message is birthed into the world with Good News. Like Mary gave birth to Jesus, the church ushers in the Gospel message concerning Jesus, God's answer to the human predicament. Here it is—*"In Christ, God was reconciling the world to himself, not counting their trespasses against them"* (2 Corinthians 5:19, NKJV). The relationship between God and man is severely broken and disrupted. There is a wide chasm between the holy God and sinful humanity. It is farther than the east is from the west, making reconciliation impossible outside of Divine intervention. Only in and through Christ could the holy God reconcile the world to Himself. It is Christ alone that makes man's reconciliation possible. The narrowness of Christianity is found in the fact that only Jesus Christ qualifies as the sinless sin offering (Hebrews 9:11-14). The only way we can come to God is through the blood of His Son (Hebrews 9:22). The way to God is a bloody way. It is not through your blood, but His Son's blood. *"For our sake he made him to be sin who knew no sin, so that in him we might become the righteousness of God"* (2 Corinthians 5:21, ESV). The Gospel we share with the world is that God made Jesus our sin bearer. He took our sins to the cross and there He substituted for us, becoming our vicarious sufferer and paying our debt. He paid it in full, completely. He not only paid the debt, He also released us from the bondage of sin, making us the righteousness of God. We are now representatives of His kingdom of righteousness (see Mathew 6:33; Romans 6:18). We will look at this responsive reality later.

The world is the focus of the reconciling work of God in Christ. Universalism is not what is taught here. Even though reconciliation is made possible through Jesus' atoning act, it is not automatic. Jesus was and is the gift to the entire world as expressed in John 3:16; but the entire world will not become the recipients of the gift. Although the world is the object of the gift of God's love, they will not all become the heirs of salvation. He desires the reconciliation of all, however, all will not response positively to His love (2 Peter 3:9). All those elected in Christ will respond as a matter of grace through faith. Nonetheless, we bear the message of hope for the world. There is hope in Jesus Christ and Him alone.

> *"My hope is built on nothing less than Jesus' blood and righteousness; I dare not trust the sweetest frame, but wholly lean on Jesus' name.*
>
> *When darkness veils His lovely face, I rest on His unchanging grace; in every high and stormy gale my anchor holds within the veil.*
>
> *His oath, His covenant, His blood support me in the whelming flood; when all around my soul gives way, He then is all my hope and stay.*
>
> *When He shall come with trumpet sound, O may I then in Him be found, dressed in His righteousness alone, faultless to stand before the throne.*
>
> *On Christ, the solid Rock, I stand—all other ground is sinking sand, all other ground is sinking sand."*[29]

The church is the best gift to the world when she majors in the ministry of reconciliation. This is majoring in the Gospel ministry. We diminish our giftedness in the world when we do not focus on Christ and Him crucified (2 Corinthians 1:18-25). When we fail to major in the Gospel ministry, we announce that we are ashamed of the Gospel (Romans 1:16). Do we count the Cross as foolishness? Is this the reason we don't major in the ministry of reconciliation? We best serve the world through the preaching of the Gospel (see Romans 1:14-15; 1 Corinthians 2:1-5). The Gospel ministry is the business of the entire church, both lay and clergy (Acts 8:4). We have been given the ministry of reconciliation. It is a gift given to us to be a gift to the world concerning Jesus Christ, the greatest gift ever given. The entire church is the community of the reconciled. Those who have experienced reconciliation are given the ministry and word of reconciliation. It is the ministry of spreading the Gospel into the entire world (Acts 1:8). The church has not been faithful to Christ, the Sender, if the Gospel ministry is not the motive of all that she does. The church has not been faithful if the Gospel ministry is the business of only the few, and not all. The primary purpose for the church's existence is to reconcile men to God. As God was in Christ reconciling the world to Himself, Christ is in His church reconciling the world through the ministry and word of reconciliation. Reconciliation happens only in Christ and through His church, both are exclusive places. Only the reconciler and the reconciled are qualified for this ministry of reconciliation. What Christ did was objective reconciliation. What the church does is subjective. In the historical sense, Christ has reconciled the world through His atoning act on the cross; but through the ministry of the church, it is presented to the world for acceptance or rejection. This is the message of the church to the world, *"We implore you on behalf of Christ, be reconciled to God"* (2 Corinthians 5:20).

Jesus' vision and strategy for His church as a gift to the world was to go and make disciples of all nations (Matthew 28:19-20). His vision and strategy must become ours. The disciple-making vision and strategy is the Gospel shared in the context of relationships. A Christianity that is not relational like the Christ of Christianity was, is not Christianity. In Christ, God reveals Himself and shared Himself with man (John 1:14). The church was not designed to live life in the worship center, rather in the world, the marketplace of life. The Gospel preached on Sunday must become portable, personal, practical, and powerful. The church has not been sent to do business in the gathering place, but in the marketplace. Therefore, the church is at her best when she scatters. In reality, the church does not need a building to do what Christ told her to do, rather she needs obedient followers of Christ, relating, reflecting, and reproducing disciples in their concentric circle of influence.

The apostle Paul reminds us in 2 Corinthians 4:1 that when we engage in the ministry of reconciliation, we are entrusted with "this" ministry. The adjective "this" modifies the noun ministry. It is a demonstrative adjective, in the accusative case of limitation. Therefore, we must not be involved in these ministries, but only "this" ministry. We should limit our focus to "this" ministry. We must save our strength for "this" ministry. We must fix our minds on "this" ministry. As a matter of fact, it is the subtle trap of the devil to busy the church in doing good things in order to divert her from "this" ministry to the world—the reconciling gospel. This does not mean that ancillary, minor ministries do not have significance, like home and foreign missions, benevolent ministries, life stages ministries, and social ministries. Rather all the minor and ancillary ministries must lead to the major ministry of reconciling the world back to God through making, marking, maturing, and multiplying disciples. The greatest danger in this pluralistic world is a pluralistic church. The world desires a universalistic church that is suggested in pluralism. A wide-open church with no standards of righteousness has a better chance of experiencing numerical growth, than a kingdom of righteousness church that focuses on "this" ministry of reconciling the world to God through Jesus Christ.

This chapter is related to the previous chapter concerning the business of the church; it overlaps in scope. However, in this chapter, I want us to understand that the church exists for the sake of the world. The church is sent to transact the business of the kingdom in the kingdom of darkness. The church and her members are sent into the world as ambassadors on the mission of hope. We represent Christ. We come from another world with a message of good news for a bad news world, telling the world that your sins have been transferred to Christ's account. "*He who knew no sin for your sake was made sin, so that in Him you might become the righteousness of God*" (2 Corinthians 5:21). But God in Christ not only remits and redeems but regenerates. As Christ's ambassadors, we represent Him in principle and presence. In the old creation, we were fallen in Adam, now we are the new creation raised in the Second Adam. The ambassadorship expressed in 2 Corinthians 5:20 is related to the new creation stated in (2 Corinthians 5:17). The body of Christ and the members therein are citizen of heaven (Philippians 3:20). Peter says that we are strangers and aliens (1 Peter 2:11). The church and her members are new in kind. They possess a resurrection quality of life (Romans 6:4-11). The resurrection of Jesus Christ is more than historical and eschatological, it is an existential reality of the new life in the believer. Eternal life is the life of tomorrow lived in the now. It is the quality of the resurrection experienced now, looking forward to the resurrection of the body. Although, the apostle Paul has believers in mind that are individually new creatures, they represent a collective community of the new creation, the new humanity, the new man. It is a colony of aliens and strangers. It is the good news community of proclamation and demonstration.

As Christ's gift to the world, the church offers hope to the world. The church and her members remain in the world as demonstrative hope. We are declarative hope in that we are a new creature in an older sinful ordered world. The power of demonstrative and the declarative hope is found in what we were, and in what we have become, and in what we are becoming (see John 5:24; Romans 6:15-23; 1 Corinthians 6:9-11; Ephesians 2:1-5; Colossians 2:13). Hope is discovered in our past tenseness. We were dead, but now we are alive; we were lost, but now we are found; we were an old self, but now we are a new self; we were darkness, but now we are light; we have passed from death to life in Christ. The hope that we offer is found on the other side of the grave—the Resurrection. The miracle in the midst of misery and the mess of life, is the Gospel that brings deliverance (Romans 1:16). As the gift of hope, we must always be prepared to give a defense to the world's inquiry concerning this hope they see in the community of hope (1 Peter 3:15). This hope is found in our counter distinction from the world, and the difference is the abundant life, the victorious life, the overcoming life. It is living on a higher plane. It is the life of Christ lived by the power of the Holy Spirit in ordinary people rendering them extra-ordinary (1 John 5:11-12). The Spirit-filled life is the source of our expression of hope in a hopeless world (see Romans 8:9-11; Ephesians 5:18). The church and her members are gifts of hope to the world. If we are to be hope, we cannot conform to the world. Our hope is in living a transformed life (Romans 12:1-2). Our hope in the world is being salt in the earth and light in the world (Matthew 5:13-16). Our hope in the world is being witnesses of Christ (Acts 1:8). Our hope in the world is found in our specificity (1 Peter 2:9-12). There is no hope in carnality, only in spirituality. There is no hope in forms of godliness (2 Timothy 3:5).

The church is a blessing to the world for we are "hope dealers," as said by Dr. Jerry Young, pastor of the New Hope Baptist Church of Jackson, Mississippi, and president of the National Baptist Convention, USA, Incorporated. We not only *preach* hope, but we *are* hope. *"But sanctify the Lord in your hearts, and always be ready to give a defense to everyone who asks you a reason for the hope that is in you, with meekness and fear"* (1 Peter 3:15, NKJV). The amazing thing about the church is that she exists for non-members of the body of Christ. Focusing on meeting the real needs of non-members of the body rather than the felt needs is paramount to the business of the church. Jesus said, "Bread but not bread alone" (Matthews 4:4). This is what Jesus said to Satan when He was being tempted. There is much more to life than the material and physical—there is the spiritual. The Word of God is the spiritual for the spiritual life; therefore, spiritual birth is needed more so in the world than the stuff of life and the cares of life. The things of this world profit little compared to the wellness of the soul (Matthew 16:26). As hope dealers, we must be cognitive of the value of a soul, the very essence of man. That which will endure death, transcending time, and will raise up in eternal life with God or apart from Him. It is true what Ezekiel says: *"The soul who sins shall die,"* (Ezekiel 18:20, ESV) but not in annihilation. The soul lives on in eternity in God's presence or His absence. We must not place more value in time than we do in eternity (Romans 8:18). Bread, but not bread alone. The social, but moreover, the spiritual, that which is related to God who is Spirit Person.

There is much discussion in light of the current pandemic brought on by the coronavirus in giving the peoples of the world hope. However, since the first Adam, the most devastating pandemic in human history is sin (Romans 5:12). Ultimately speaking, even this virus is the result of sin. If death entered the world because of sin, certainly sickness and disease are the result of sin. Sin brought death and everything that results in death. How does a bear, in hibernation live on? It lives on hope of the coming spring. What would we be without hope? In the midst of this devastating pandemic, we are looking for hope for a better day. For the Christian, hope is not wishful thinking, but the certainty of a reality not yet experienced. It is hope in God. Hope for a better day, hope for a positive outcome, hope for the dawning of a new day, but God is the object of our hope (see Psalms 33:18; 39:7; 43:5; 71:5; 119:114; Jeremiah 29:11; Lamentation 3:24; Romans 8:24-25; 15:13; Colossians 1:27; Hebrews 10:23). Hope in God is trusting His will for the present and the future (Romans 8:28). It is not hope in man, who only sees the parade, one frame at a time, but hope in God, who sees the whole parade in one glance. We hope in God who holds our destiny in His hands. Hope in God, who has purpose for us, as we walk in His purpose. Hope is the positive expectation of the future. As hope, we are the people of the future living in the now. We are the community of the not yet, living in the now. We have eternal life, tomorrow's life, lived in the present. We are the people of the eschaton living in the existential. We are the "Easter" people responding in resurrection hope, because our Lord is the resurrection and the life (John 11:25). Easter people have already experienced resurrection, spiritually, with certainty of physical resurrection in the eschaton (see Romans 6:4-5; 1 Corinthians 15:35-49).

The church exists for the world. She is the hope for the world. Loyal only to Christ and His mandate, but for the sake of the world. As Christ was the hope of the world. The church is now the hope for and in the world. As hope she must have voice and visibility. As hope dealers, we must live in contrast to the world. *"But sanctify the Lord God in your hearts"* (1 Peter 3:15). We live "instead of" lives. "Instead of" being afraid, we are affirmed. "Instead of" being troubled, we are triumphant in trouble. In hopelessness, we are hopeful. In tribulation we don't renege, we rejoice. Our witness is in our contrast. Our hope for the world is in living in contrast to the world. We experience like all, the vicissitudes and enigmas of life, but differently—with hope in God. Our witness to the world is in how we handle reversals and adversities. Can God trust us with sufferings for His name's sake and glory? Like, the ancient Job, can we say, "Though he slays me, I will hope in him" (Job 13:15, ESV). Only saints can sanctify the Lord God in their hearts. Our true identity is we are saints, not sinners. We were sinners, now we are saints that are sinning less, as we grow in sanctification (1 Corinthians 6:11). As hope dealers, we live consecrated lives. Having been set apart for God's purpose as saints. We are not perfect, but simply set apart for God's use. Our sainthood is our position in Christ (Ephesians 1:1). We are not saints in the future, rather we are saints now. Our qualification in becoming saints, is not miracles attributed to us, but miracles that Christ has accomplished through regeneration. I believe, Paul's self-identification as the chief of sinners (1 Timothy 1:15) refers his past treatment of Christians before he became a Christian. In his estimation, his record has never been surpassed, so he felt that he still holds the record as chief sinner. Therefore, if he could be saved by grace, anyone could be saved by grace, for he was the chief sinner. I really think that Satan holds that record as chief sinner (John 8:44). For the essence of sin is lying about who He is.

We are hope as God's possessions. He is Lord. We are His slaves. Once we were runaway slaves, but in Christ we have returned. We are saints because of His ownership of us. In our obedience to the Gospel, there is surrendering faith. Not mere cognitive faith. There is surrendering to the Lordship of Jesus Christ. There is inward submitting. We give up our rights to our lives (1 Corinthians 6:19-20). Our freedom to be who we were created to be is surrendering our freedom to become Christ's slaves. What a paradox (Matthew 10:39; Mark 8:35). We do not make Him Lord. He became Lord without our vote and approval. It happened in faith. If Christ is resident in you, He is Lord, for God has made Him so (Acts 2:36; Romans 14:9; Philippians 2:11). What authority do we have to make Him Lord? He is Lord just like He is Savior. We did not make Him Savior. In our trusting Him as Savior He became also Lord. If He is in your life, He is Lord of your life. As saints, we live in the will of God. Faith is actually saying yes. While sin is actually saying no. All of this happens inwardly. It is a matter of the heart which includes the mind, the will, and the emotions.

Hope dealers are *"prepared to give an answer to everyone who asks you to give the reason for the hope that is in you"* (1 Peter 3:15). Our fundamental preparedness is the reality of our position in Christ. We reside in hope, and hope resides in us. We are positive people, prepared people, peculiar people, and pardoned people. We are called to live in response mode. Always on duty for a defense of the Gospel of grace. What do we need to do to be ready? We need to know the hope that is in the Gospel. Know the faith concerning the Gospel. Know the human predicament and what it means to be lost. Know the bad news in order to share the Good News. We are to be apologists—defenders of the faith. Apologetics is giving answers which come from the word *apology*, but not being sorry. We are not ashamed of the Gospel. It is to do with knowing the Gospel and being the Gospel. Know and be known by the Gospel. We are able because of exposition and experiential of the Gospel to be hope in the world. We do not argue and debate the Gospel. We simply declare the truth of the Scriptures, concerning Jesus Christ, who is the personification of the Gospel, and then demonstrate it through the newness of life. The hope is in being music and then lyrics. However, music is preceded by poetry (in the beginning was the word, and word became flesh) the poetry became music. His workmanship (poetry) with lyrics, the reincarnation of the Word made flesh. We are music in the major key, not in the minor key. In the delightful key and not the doleful keys. The major key of hope, and not the minor key in hopelessness.

Hope dealers communicate hope in the Lord Jesus. In making the defense, we give answers for the hope we possess in Christ. We answer the query, "What would I have if I had Jesus?" There is the cry for the pragmatic and personification of hope. The world wants to see hope in us. What difference would it make in my life if I had Jesus in my life? We are to become answers to hopelessness. What is the rationale for our certainty? Post-modern thought says there are no certainties or absolutes—all is subjective. Is there hope for me? Soren Kierkegaard thought that "truth and things that really matter in life are not objective. They are subjective." Nietzsche said, "Consider morals as well as truth to be relative." This is against the biblical view and even modernism. In postmodernism, to claim to be the answer or to have the answer is arrogance, for everything is subjective and uncertain. Yes! We are answers to hope. Can Jesus raise the dead? Can Jesus save the lost? Can Jesus transform lives? Can Jesus undo what sin has done to us? The four lepers in 2 Kings were the answer to the problem in Samaria. Lazarus was the answer to death. How can a man be justified before a holy and righteous God? As answers, we are evidence of His power. We make a defense before the unbelieving world concerning the truth of the Gospel. Our apologetic is not one of apologies, rather the appropriating of the Gospel in declaration and demonstration.

As answers, we serve as hosts. Like antibodies host fighting age agents for the coronavirus, we are hope for the sin virus that is pandemic in our world. There is a correlation between the coronavirus and sin. This virus is like sin. It is global and deadly, so is sin. The virus is an infectious disease, so is sin infectious and pandemic. There are resemblances between the virus and sin, but the resultant consequence is different. The virus can lead to physical death, but sin leads to physical, spiritual, and eternal death, known in the Bible as the second death. Thank God for His healing mercies through miracles and medical professionals that extend time for all, but especially for those not prepared to die and meet God in peace. Who has the spiritual antibodies? Those who have experienced death to sin. They are the ones who are spiritual antibodies. They are agents of hope, as the answers, panaceas, of the human predicament. We have the neutralized pathogens to keep sin from spreading (1 John 3:9). We hate sin and are confessors and sin fighters. The god of this world has blinded the eyes of the world so that they do not view sin as a common enemy. The antibody in the believer is the seed, the divine life (1 John 3:9). The believer is hope in the world because their antibodies hold back the spreading of sin; first in them, and then in the world.

Without a doubt, we need the Holy Spirit as our Defense Attorney to aid us in telling the truth about the Truth (Jesus), the power of the Spirit of Truth (see John 16:13-15; Acts 1:8). We should always be ready to explain the hope that is with us with meekness and respect for God, who has graced us.

Chapter 7

The Building

"It isn't *a* building, but *the* building."

"Do you not know that you are God's temple and that God's Spirit dwells in you?"—1 Corinthians 3:16, ESV

The church is not a building rather it is a place where the church assembles for corporate worship and biblical instructions. It is the central place for equipping the saints for the work of the ministry and reaching the world with the Gospel of grace. After saying this, I must also say that the church, the people of God, do not need a building to do what God in Christ has commanded the church to be and to do. We must note here that centuries passed before the church had a building to gather in. And yet it was engaged in reaching the world with the Gospel. We have already discussed that the church was sent to do business in the world. It was and is to be missional and not stationary. The church was called to be the diaspora. Listen to Jesus:

> *"As you sent me into the world, so I have sent them into the world"* (John 17:18, ESV).

> *"Go therefore and make disciples of all nations, baptizing them in the name of the Father and of the Son and of the Holy Spirit"* (Matthew 28:19, ESV).

> *"You will receive power when the Holy Spirit has come upon you, and you will be my witnesses in Jerusalem and in all Judea and Samaria, and to the end of the earth"* (Acts 1:8, ESV).

The church cannot obey the mandate of the Master and not be missional. But she had to be pushed by persecution to become mobile.

> *"Now Saul was consenting to his death. At that time a great persecution arose against the church which was at Jerusalem; and they were all scattered throughout the regions of Judea and Samaria, except the apostles. And devout men carried Stephen to his burial and made great lamentation over him. As for Saul, he made havoc of the church, entering every house, and dragging off men and women, committing them to prison. Therefore, those who were scattered went everywhere preaching the word"* (Acts 8:1-4, NKJV).

The significance of the death of Stephen is causation of the mission thrust of the Gospel, the church went beyond Jerusalem; and the apostles and others preached or evangelized in the world. But we must also note that Stephen was stoned to death, becoming the primary martyr of the church because he challenged their temple theology.

> *"Our fathers had the tabernacle of witness in the wilderness, as He appointed, instructing Moses to make it according to the pattern that he had seen, which our fathers, having receive it in turn, also brought with Joshua into the land possessed by the Gentiles, whom God drove out before the face of our fathers until the day of David, who found favor before God and asked to find a dwelling for the God of Jacob. But Solomon built Him a house. However, the Most High does not dwell in temples made with hands, as the prophet says; 'Heaven is My throne, and the earth is My footstool. What house will you build for Me? Says the Lord,*

or what is the place of My rest? Has My hand did not make all these things'" (Acts 7:44-50, NKJV).

The Tabernacle and the Temple were the symbolic presence of God. He never lived or existed in those ancient symbolic structures. However, there is much to be learned and appreciated in the detail splendor of the architectural design from without and from within. It was places that bespoke the holiness of God. Everything in the Tabernacle and Temple was sacred. For instance, unauthorized touching of the Ark, that would later be part of the Tabernacle and Temple, would bring death (Numbers 4:15). The apostle Paul announced to the Christians in Corinth that not only are they saints, but they are the sanctuary of the Holy Spirit, both individually and corporately.

> *"To the church of God, which is at Corinth, to those who are sanctified in Christ Jesus, called to be saints"* (1 Corinthians 1:2, NKJV).

> *"Do you not know that your body is the temple of the Holy Spirit who is in you, whom you have from God, and you are not your own?* (1 Corinthians 6:19, NKJV).

> *"Do you not know that you are the temple of God and that the Spirit of God dwells in you?"* (1 Corinthians 3:16, NKJV).

Although this is metaphoric language, it is the spiritual reality of the believer. As saints, the believer is the sanctuary, the temple, the house, and the edifice of God. If you please, saints are also holy ground, the sacred society of the saints, the dwelling place of the Holy Spirit, corporately and then individually. Peter, the little rock represented the nature of every believer, *"living stones built into a spiritual house"* (1 Peter 2:5, ESV). Jesus announced the essence of the church when He said, *"And I tell you, you are Peter, and on this rock, I will build my church, and the gates of hell shall not prevail against it"* (Matthew 16:18, ESV). It is obvious that Jesus is the Rock, and we and Peter are little rocks corresponding to the nature of the Head of the church. Jesus would build His church of those who have His nature.

The advent of the Holy Spirit into the world and Jesus' promise that He will be with us always (Matthew 28:20) is associated with the presence of the Holy Spirit and the nature of Jesus in the believer. The advent is His special presence in the church and the Christian. Although He is omnipresent, He is particularly present in us. We will speak more concerning the Spirit in the last chapter of the book. The Owner of the church and Lord of the Christian resides in the building that He is building. He does not rent it out for others to live in it. He takes up occupancy in His Own dwelling. This is mystery, miracle and marvelous, rendering the church glorious. It is the greater of the One who is resident in us that makes the church glorious.

> *"He put all things under his feet and gave him as head over all things to the church, which is his body, the fullness of him who fills all in all"* (Ephesians 1:22-23, ESV).

We place more emphasis on the building that houses the church than on the church in the physical structure. We honor the place where the church meets more than the saints in the place. We forbid certain things not to take place in the structure and condone ungodly behavior and conduct inside of the saints and the sanctuary of the living church. This is what Paul was addressing in 1 Corinthians 3. He was reminding them that they were fellow workers, God's field and His building, but were destroying the fellowship and purpose therein with childlike behavior, frivolous works, partisanship, and ungodly wisdom destroying the fellowship and purpose God will judge. This destruction is rendering the church inoperative. This certainly can happen through false teachers and teaching. Those who teach and preach in the church of Jesus Christ need to realize the holiness of the Word of God and the people of God. We are stewards of that which is holy. Like the priests and the Levites were stewards of the symbolic presence of God—the Tabernacle and the Temple, every believer is a steward of the physical body wherein Holy Spirit dwells, and the visible church, a microcosm of the invisible church. We are living sanctuaries. The songwriter in prayerful fashion said, *"Lord, prepare me to be a sanctuary, pure and holy, tried and true; with thanksgiving, I'll be a living sanctuary for you."*[30] It seem to be inspired by Psalm 15:1-5:

> *"Lord, who may abide in Your tabernacle? Who may dwell in Your holy hill? He who walks uprightly, and works righteousness, and speaks the truth in his heart; he who does not backbite with his tongue, nor does evil to his neighbor, nor does he take up a reproach against his friend; in whose eyes a vile person is despised, but he honors those who fear the Lord; he who swears to his own hurt and does not change; he who does not put out his money at usury, nor does he take a bribe against the innocent. He who does these things shall never be moved"* (NKJV).

This speaks of those abiding in the holy Tabernacle must correspond in holiness. But, moreover, we are speaking of the Holy One abiding in us. What makes us holy is the Holy Spirit in us. Surely, we are in Christ and Christ is in us (John 17:23-26). Sainthood requires evidence of a miracle done to enter this elite crowd, but so in Scripture, sainthood comes to those who are miracles in regeneration (Ephesians 1:1-14). We are saints in the process of sanctification towards glorification (Philippians 1:6; 2:12-13). Sainthood is not reserved for that day. It is our reality now. We have been set apart unto Him. He is already at home in us making us saints because of where He is and where we are—in Him (Colossians 1:27).

It is wrong to think of our church buildings as sanctuaries. It is unchristian and borders on paganism. We are the temple wherein God dwells; therefore, our relationships ought not to be mis-mated with unbelievers, darkness, and idolatry. The holy must not be related to the profane. The believer's heart is the inner sanctuary where God is present, not in symbolism but in spiritual actuality. Sense Christian marriage is holy unto the Lord, it should not be mis-mated—unequally yoked.

> *"Do not be unequally yoked with unbelievers. For what partnership has righteousness with lawlessness? Or what fellowship has light with darkness? What accord has Christ with Belial? Or what portion does a believer share with an unbeliever? What agreement has the temple of God with idols? For we are the temple of the living God; as God said, "I will make my dwelling among them and walk among them, and I will be their God, and they shall be my people. Therefore, go out from their midst, and be separate from them, says the Lord, and touch no unclean thing; then I will welcome you, and you shall be sons and daughters to me, says the Lord Almighty"'* (2 Corinthians 6:14-18, ESV).

Chapter 8

The Bride

"Here comes the bride."

"I feel a divine jealousy for you, since I betrothed you to one husband, to present you as a pure virgin to Christ."—2 Corinthians 11:2, ESV

> *"Husbands, love your wives, as Christ loved the church and gave himself up for her, that he might sanctify her, having cleansed her by the washing of water with the word, so that he might present the church to himself in splendor, without spot or wrinkle or any such thing, that she might be holy and without blemish."*—Ephesians 5:25-27, ESV

> *"Let us rejoice and exult and give him the glory, for the marriage of the Lamb has come, and his Bride has made herself ready."*—Revelation 19:7, ESV

The metaphor Bride and Bridegroom should not be minimized. The metaphor of marriage is of tremendous importance as it tells of the Trinity, Christian marriage and the glorious church. The Bride and the Bridegroom announce plural oneness. As it points to the mystery of marriage in heaven that is to be demonstrated on earth through Christian marriages. Here again we see the purposeful God working out His plan on earth as it is to be in heaven at the Marriage Feast of the Lamb. Please note that there is mentioned the "bride and then the bridegroom." There is the matter of distinction—there is wife and there is husband in the idea of bride and groom. No two wives and no two husbands are to form or define marriage. It is to be "hetero" difference in sameness.

It is very important that damage is not done to the theology of the mystery of the Trinity. Listen to this mystery language at the dawn of creation:

> *"God said, 'Let Us make man in Our image, according to Our likeness; let them have dominion over the fish of the sea, over the birds of the air, and over the cattle, over all the earth and over every creeping thing that creeps on the earth.' So God created man in His own image; in the image of God He created him; male and female He created them"* (Genesis 1:26-27, NKJV).

The mystery is found in the Trinitarian oneness revealed in the "us-ness" in the passage. The monotheistic God speaks of Himself in plural oneness making the image and likeness of God in mankind plural oneness—male and female. Watch this marvelous truth as there is a holy society in the Godhead, there is also a holy society in humanity. While there is sameness in essence, there is distinction in persons, and so must there be in humanity and, therefore, in marriage. This is basic to the meaning of mankind being created in the image of God—plural oneness. There is also the understanding of image-bearing as self-determination, self-consciousness and moral consciousness, distinguishing man's existence directly from the Creator and some evolutionary process of man evolving from the unintelligent protozoan or primate. If there is any idea of evolution, it is that man did not come from the ape, but away from the ape, leaving it in the jungle and zoo, while man landed on the moon and traveled to Mars. In my feeble estimation, it is nonsensical to think that unintelligent can produce intelligence.

The idea of the Trinity is derived from Scripture. The term *Trinity* is not found in Scripture, but the truth of Trinity is declared in the sacred text of Scripture. Not to believe in plural oneness is to leave you exposed to some form of polytheism—many gods, or modalism—God engaged in roleplaying. Don't miss the Trinitarian theology in the following passage:

> *"Go therefore and make disciples of all nations, baptizing them in **the name** of the Father and the Son and of the Holy Spirit"* (Matthew 28:19, ESV).

Baptizing in the one name denotes oneness of the plural Godhead. This is not roleplaying. The Father, the Son, and the Holy Spirit are distinct Persons of the Trinity, and even before creation they existed in this holy society called Trinity. We saw this in Genesis 1:26 in the "let us in our own image" declarative.

This God who is relational within Himself created humanity to engage in relationship with man on earth as He relates to Himself in heaven. This was so until man chose to rebel against God and live independent of God which is a form of humanism. It was a type of divorcement from God. It was idolatrous and adulterous because the relationship was broken.

> *"All we like sheep have gone astray; we have turned—everyone to his own way; and the L*ORD *has laid on him the iniquity of us all"* (Isaiah 53:6, ESV).

The fact the God sought Adam and Eve in the Garden of Eden let us know that there was a relationship between God and our primal parents, and their sins separated them from their loving God (Isaiah 59:2).

It is clear in Scripture that the nation Israel was in a marital, covenant relationship with God. Being religious is never the will of God. It is all about relationships with God.

> *"They say, 'If a man divorces his wife, and she goes from him and becomes another man's, may he return to her again?' Would*

not that land be greatly polluted? But you have played the harlot with many lovers; yet return to Me,' says the LORD" (Jeremiah 3:1, NKJV).

"Bring charges against your mother, bring charges; for she is not My wife, nor am I her Husband! Let her put away her harlotries from her sight, and her adulteries from between her breasts; lest I strip her naked and expose her, as in the day she was born, and make her like a wilderness, and set her like a dry land, and slay her with thirst. I will not have mercy on her children, for they are the children of harlotry" (Hosea 2:2-4, NKJV).

Israel was in a relationship with God. God had chosen them to be His covenant people wherein He would bless the whole world (Genesis 12:1-3). But as seen in the life of the prophet Hosea and his wife Gomer, Israel was unfaithful, becoming an adulterous nation. Now sin is always against God. Yes, against His laws and righteousness, but ultimately against who He is (Psalm 51:4). Unbelievers and sinners commit sins outside the relationship (a type of fornication in nature), but the believer and saints commit sins inside the relationship (a type of adultery in nature). Sinners sin against the law and righteousness of God but not against their relationship for they have none. They sin against the "who" of God for the moral law denotes the character of God as does the righteousness standards of God does. However, the saint sins inside their relationship with God. Children are sinning against the Father, while the children of darkness only sin against the Creator.

In a real sense, marriage is meant for the godly and not the ungodly. For God instituted marriage as a reflection of His Trinitarian existence. This intra-Trinitarians reality is to be lived out in the fact that the two shall become one flesh. Marriage can only take place as hetero become homogeneous. The two shall become one marital person. It is marriage because the others have become the same. You cannot marry yourself.

There is not leaving and cleaving in sameness. Eve came from Adam, but remarkably different, compatible and capable of reproduction (Genesis 1:27-28).

Now the glorious church is designed to be composed of mostly Christian marriages. This is not to say that singles and the unmarried are not called to be a part of the body of Christ. But when you understand that in Christian marriage the husband and wife are roleplaying, it calls for the husband and wife to be in relationship with Christ.

> *"You say, 'Why does he not?' Because the LORD was witness between you and the wife of your youth, to whom you have been faithless, though she is your companion and your wife by covenant. Did he not make them one, with a portion of the Spirit in their union? And what was the one God seeking? Godly offspring. So, guard yourselves in your spirit, and let none of you be faithless to the wife of your youth. For the man who does not love his wife but divorces her, says the LORD, the God of Israel, covers his garment with violence, says the LORD of hosts. So guard yourselves in your spirit, and do not be faithless"* (Malachi 2:14-16, ESV).

This roleplaying is vividly seen in Ephesians 5:22-33, where the husband plays the role of Christ and the wife plays the role of the church. It presupposes Christians are acting out the roles. For the husband cannot love like Christ without the nature of Christ and the wife cannot submit to her husband without submitting to Christ in salvation. And all of this is made possible when the Spirit is in control (Ephesians 5:18). The Holy Spirit can only reign where He resides (Romans 8:9-11). Marriage is meant for most because of the sexual drive within humanity, and the only divine context for the expression and experience of sexual intercourse is in marriage (Hebrew 13:4). Outside of marriage, God prohibits coitus. Therefore, marriage is God's purpose for most of us. However, we must be cognitive of the basic purpose for marriage, an image of the

Trinity—plural oneness.

The church as the Bride of Christ indicates the importance of marriage on earth as an illustration of the marriage that will take place in heaven. At this present time, the church is engaged to Christ. The presence of the Holy Spirit in the life of the believer and church is evidence of the pre-marriage commitment. As Joseph and Mary were engaged, Joseph was told not to divorce her because she, as virgin, was pregnant due to the Holy Spirit, so is Christ and His church espoused and there can be no divorce for it would contradict the reality of the Trinity and the witness of the church and Christian marriages. This is one of the main reason God hates divorce. It is untruth concerning Him in plural oneness. The Holy Trinity will never be separated in essence (Matthew 27:46). The cry of Jesus on the cross of God's forsakenness is not divorce taking place in the Godhead, rather God's judgment of sin in Jesus our sin bearer. God abandoned Jesus in order reconcile us through His blood. For God to rescue Him would be to abandon the sinner forever. God was abandoning Jesus for He had laid on Him the iniquities of us all (Isaiah 53:6; 2 Corinthians 5:21). In becoming sin for us, the Son of God did not cease being the Son. The fellowship with the Father was interrupted. We hear Jesus referring to the Father as God and not Father, the relational title, because He was in substitutional mode. John MacArthur said, "By the incarnation itself there already had been a partial separation. Because Jesus had been separated from His divine glory and from face-to-face communication with the Father, refusing to hold on to those divine privileges for His own sake."[31]

Here comes the Bride! As Hosea had to retrieve Gomer as his wife, so Christ as aforementioned paid for His Bride, the church (Acts 20:28). Jesus had stated that He was going away to prepare a place for His Bride (John 14:1-4). He had to go through Calvary and the grave to prepare for the upcoming wedding. The glorious church is seen in the Bride metaphor. This special relationship as Bride is the church of Jesus Christ with invited guest at the Marriage Feast of the Lamb. The Old Testament saints and perhaps the tribulation saints will be celebratory guests when Christ presents the church as His Bride.

> *"So that he might present the church to himself in splendor, without spot or wrinkle or any such thing, that she might be holy and without blemish"* (Ephesians 5:27, ESV).

Christ has designed to begin the presenting of His church in splendor, without spot or wrinkle or any such thing, holy and without blemish on earth through the ministry of marriage. It happens in the disposition of the husband loving his wife as Christ loved the church and the wife respectively loving her husband as unto the Lord. This is the disposition of nurture moving from glory to glory (2 Corinthians 3:18). The sanctifying work should begin inside the Christian marriage and then through the discipleship process of the church. Remember, the purpose of marriage is for the glory of God in order to bring Him glory by participating in presenting the church in splendor, spotless, wrinkleless, and holy without blemish. The church and each member exist for His glory. This is the primary purpose of the church in the world, and the secondary purpose is the ministry of reconciling the world starting with marriage and the family and beyond (see 1 Corinthians 10: 31; 2 Corinthians 5:18-19).

The roleplay of the husband is a tremendous responsibility for it is aligned with Jesus' sacrifice and self-giving of Himself. The role is not something to be sought after and envied. It demands coming to the end of self for the sake of the wife and the health of the Bride of Christ. Yes! I did say that the husband's role in the marriage will affect the health of the church both the visible and invisible church.

> *"Wives submit to your own husbands, as to the Lord. For the husband is the head of the wife even as Christ is the head of the church, his body, and is himself its Savior. Now as the church*

submits to Christ, so also wives should submit in everything to their husbands. Husbands love your wives, as Christ loved the church and gave himself up for her, that he might sanctify her, having cleansed her by the washing of water with the word, so that he might present the church to himself in splendor, without spot or wrinkle or any such thing, that she might be holy and without blemish. In the same way husbands should love their wives as their own bodies. He who loves his wife loves himself. For no one ever hated his own flesh, but nourishes and cherishes it, just as Christ does the church, because we are members of his body. Therefore, a man shall leave his father and mother and hold fast to his wife, and the two shall become one flesh. This mystery is profound, and I am saying that it refers to Christ and the church. However, let each one of you love his wife as himself, and let the wife see that she respects her husband" (Ephesians 5:22-33, ESV).

The husband is to be Christlike in the marriage in particular. He is to love like Christ, to submit like Christ, sacrifice like Christ, and serve like Christ. These Christlikenesses are expressions of love. Paul was revolutionary in that he spoke of husbands loving their wives. Wives were like property in that world system. They were owned. They were above slaves and animals but not equal to men. It was a patriarchal system never intended by the Creator to be domineering and demeaning towards women and wives (Genesis 1:26-31). There were to be roles of responsibility from the beginning (see 1 Corinthians 11:1-10; Colossians 3:18-19). This reducing womanhood and wives to inequality with men and husbands is a matter of sin. Unfortunately, this sinful behavior still exists in these modern days due to sin and not God.

However, in the new humanity and in the life of the body of Christ, the husband is to act like Christ towards women and his wife in particular. He is to love like Christ who loved His church. How did He love the church, His Bride to be? He gave Himself to her. He did not give her things, but Himself. He would give His life for her, but He gave Himself before He gave His life for her. Please don't miss this. He surrendered who He was to her. The church had Him. Christ submitted Himself to the Father and then to the church. As we will notice, there is to be mutual submission in marriage (Ephesians 5:21). In submission, Christ volunteered Himself to be the sacrifice. Like Isaac obeyed his father Abraham and laid down on the alter (Genesis 22:9-14), so Jesus hung on the Cross in obedience to the Father. When a wife knows she has the heart of her husband, it makes a tremendous difference in the marriage, generating her respect and submission to his role of responsibility. I want Mike Mason to speak to us right here:

> *"If people understood exactly how radical the curtailment of independence in marriage is, there could never be any thought of divorce. Divorce would be seen as a form of suicide. But then, if people understood the true depth of self-abnegation that marriage demands, there would perhaps be far fewer weddings. For marriage, too, would be seen as a form of suicide. It would be seen not as a way of augmenting one's comfort and security in life, but rather as a way of losing one's life for the sake of Christ."* [32]

In Christ-type love, the husband loves his wife by serving her, not lording over her, but stooping to wash her feet like Christ washed the feet of His disciples, declaring that, *"He did not come to be served, but to serve, and to give His life as a ransom for many"* (Mark 10:45, NIV). Serving, submission, and sacrifice run together in loving your wife like Christ loved His Bride to be. The reason we need severe sobriety when choosing to marry, and whom to marry, is that forming a marital person is committing mutual suicide.

The role of the wife is to submit; however, both she and her husband are to be engaged in mutual submission to the will and plan of God. She is to lovingly respect her husband's role as pioneering the marriage and family's journey towards the image of Jesus Christ. As head, his life directs the wife and children towards becoming like Jesus. Yes! She respects him, but, moreover, she respects his awesome responsibility of spiritual leadership (see Acts 20:28; 1 Peter 5:1-5). The husband is the pastor, the elder, and the bishop of his marriage and family. This is his miniature church that relates to the local congregation fundamental to the health of the body of Christ. The husband also serves as savior of his marriage and family by building an ark for the saving of his household (Hebrews 11:7) offering his family as example of the Gospel of grace to a world in need of grace. His wife respects and partners with him as the home becomes the primary place to make, mark, mature, and multiply disciples (1 Peter 3:7).

In the church of Jesus Christ, every male must be discipled to take on the awesome role of responsibility. Is it any wonder that there is an attack on the men? I have said, if you want to discover where the church focus needs to be, find out where and who Satan is concentrating on—men and marriages.

The glorious church is a matter of grace. The church that is engaged to Christ is imperfect. There are imperfections. She has been unfaithful to Christ, the Bridegroom. Sanctification is in process as she moves towards the wedding. Because of grace, the wedding has not been postponed. The invited guests have not been informed of any cancellation. Jesus promised to present her without spot or wrinkle in holiness. The espoused church is dressed at this present time in Christ's righteousness and shall stand before Him in the robe of glory. Listen to this glorious doxa:

> *"Now to Him who is able to keep you from stumbling, and to present you faultless before the presence of His glory with exceeding joy. To God our Savior, who alone is wise, be glory and majesty, dominion and power, both now and forever. Amen"* (Jude 1:24-25, NKJV).

There is grace in glory. For the church is glorious before the glorification of the saints realized in the eschaton. The Holy Spirit's presence and Christ's promise guarantees that the wedding will take place (see Ephesians 1:3-14; Matthew 28:20; Romans 8:33-39). There will be no divorce. Jesus, like Joseph, His stepfather, would not, and will not put the church away privately nor publicly. Witnesses and ambassadors for Christ and members of the church and citizens of the kingdom of God contradict this truth in marital divorce. Marital divorce is the death of the marital person, wherein the two became one. It is impossible for Christ and the Church to divorce. It is impossible for the Bride and the Bridegroom to separate. And it is impossible for the redeemed to become unredeemed, and the reconciled to be unreconciled, the born again to become unborn. The grace in the glory is *"being confident of this very thing, that He who has begun a good work in you will complete it until the day of Jesus Christ"* (Philippians 1:6, NKJV).

Chapter 9

The Bishop

"Caretakers of the body and bride of Christ."

"He gave the apostles, the prophets, the evangelists, the shepherds and teachers, to equip the saints for the work of ministry, for building up the body of Christ."—Ephesians 4:11-12, ESV

The glorious church is the visible church on earth; therefore, the bishops who are responsible for the business of the body of Christ are necessary gifts to the body. So, this chapter will concentrate on these caretakers of the local congregations of the church of Jesus Christ. It is an awesome responsibility overseeing the unfinished business of Christ on earth. The profundity of pastoring the people of God, whom He has purchased with His own blood (Acts 20:28) is sobering, for pastors are soul watchers. I believe if pastors really focused on the function of the bishop, and not the title of being called bishops, the desire to pastor might be seen as burden more than a blessing (1 Timothy 3:1). The nobility of pastoring is in the call of God. The desire is planted in the heart of the man of God from the heart of God. Therefore, pastoring is not a professional pursuit and a career choice, rather chosen of God from preaching to pastoring. It is a divine setup from eternity realized in time through the working of the Holy Spirit in the life of the man (Jeremiah 1:5). As a gift to the church, the pastor comes from God through the visible congregation.

Yes! The Holy Spirit is involved in the pastor's calling to the local church. Both people and pastor must live and function with this understanding. Although, there is salary involved, the pastor, whom the Holy Spirit appoints, is not a hireling (John 10:12-18) but stands in the tradition of Christ the Good, Great, and Glorious Shepherd (1 Peter 5:4).

Every pastor must ask himself what or who has called you to this office of bishop? Was it prosperity, prestige, power, or position? In my early days of pastoring, I did not realize the loftiness of the call to pastor. For me, to pastor a church was a dream come true. Beyond the rigors of pastoring, the hours of sermon preparation, endless hours of pastoral counseling, administrative duties, managing staff, deacons, and leaders, chairing business meetings, training leaders, being worship leader, and dealing with old infants, pastoring is overseeing each member's journey towards the image of Jesus Christ. This responsibility overwhelmed my soul as I realized the truth of the following passage of Scripture. It sobered me and has changed my pastoral ministry:

> *"My little children, for whom I am again in the anguish of childbirth until Christ is formed in you"* (Galatians 4:19, ESV).

Pastor Peter, a fellow elder, bothered me more deeply when he wrote to pastors this reminder:

> *"So, I exhort the elders among you, as a fellow elder and a witness of the sufferings of Christ, as well as a partaker in the glory that is going to be revealed: shepherd the flock of God that is among you, exercising oversight, not under compulsion, but willingly, as God would have you; not for shameful gain, but eagerly; not domineering over those in your charge, but being examples to the flock. And when the chief Shepherd appears, you will receive the unfading crown of glory"* (1 Peter 5:1-4, ESV).

Peter, one of the foundational leaders of the Lord's church, addresses pastors as key leaders of the Lord's church to preach and demonstrate the

Word of God as they live among the sheep. Yes! They are to smell like the sheep, for they are both sheep and shepherds. Sheep are led and not driven like goat and cows. This is upfront leadership in modeling behavior for the sheep to follow towards the image of Christ. The pastoral ministry is more modeling than management.

> *"Remember them which have the rule over you, who have spoken unto you the word of God: whose faith follow, considering the end of their conversion. . . . Obey them that have the rule over you, and submit yourselves: for they watch for your souls, as they that must give account, that they may do it with joy, and not with grief: for that is unprofitable for you"* (Hebrews 13:7, 17 NKJV).

Pastoral leadership is about character more than credentials and charismata. The qualifications for the bishop and his assistants are character in nature and not a bunch of skillsets.

> *"Therefore, an overseer must be above reproach, the husband of one wife, sober-minded, self-controlled, respectable, hospitable, able to teach, not a drunkard, not violent but gentle, not quarrelsome, not a lover of money. He must not be a recent convert, or he may become puffed up with conceit and fall into the condemnation of the devil. Moreover, he must be well thought of by outsiders, so that he may not fall into disgrace, into a snare of the devil"* (1 Timothy 3:2-7, ESV).

These qualifications are imperatives and not goals to be reached as one pastors, but prerequisites for the office of bishop, and when they are no longer true in the life of the pastor, discipline and healing is in order (1 Timothy 5:17-20). When grace is disgraced by the fall in pastoral leadership, there must not be ungrace where there is repentance. Now, the qualifications are not determined on a curve system. Every pastor is qualified or disqualified on his own merit. Neither are these qualifications graded, determining a passing score. These are "must be" qualifications (verse 2). It is a high calling. The health of the pastor is crucial to the health of the congregation. His character is measured by his conduct that begins in his private life and shown in his public life. I think it was said by Harvey Cox that *"whenever, there is a breakdown in the private life it unfits us for the demands of the public life."* Our conduct will reflect our character as pastors. Conduct is our walk among people in the world, as well as our walk in the work of ministry, in relationship with women, in relationship with wealth, and in relationship with words. How we as pastors walk on the horizontal will be determined by how we walk with God on the vertical. For we dare not work and function in all these other areas if we are not daily walking with God. Let it be known and obvious, like Enoch, that we walk with God (Genesis 5:24). Character is developed as we walk with God daily.

Christian character is how the bishop lives "above reproach." The pastor must not be guilty of the contempt of Christ, bring dishonor, disgrace and disrespect upon the name of Christ. As he rightly divides the Word of Truth, cutting it straight, he must not be guilty of walking crooked (2 Timothy 2:15-21) as a workman that has no shame. God's approval is not just a matter of his hermeneutics and homiletics, but his holiness. This is in Paul's admonition in Acts 20:28—*"Take heed to yourself."* Guard your character. How can the bishop oversee each member's journey towards the image of Christ without living above reproach? Paul lists areas of living above reproach for the pastors.

First, the husband of one wife. This probably is the most vulnerable area for many in the pastoral ministry. This is the call to be faithful to your wife. It must be of the heart. Fleeing adultery must be a matter of the heart and not just the hands. If the pastor is married, he must be totally committed to the one wife. In that day of pagan influences this prohibition was certainly necessary. And moreover, sense Christ has only one wife—the church—pastors must represent Him, if married, to be a one-wife husband. This is not one wife in a lifetime of pastoral ministry, rather one wife at a time. Marriage is not a biblical requirement for entering the pastoral ministry, but practicing marriage without a license is not permissible, this is sexual relationship outside of marriage (Hebrews 13:4). Men with the Pauline gift (1 Corinthians 7:1-7) are rare in pastoral ministry. Some believe that divorce and remarried man are prohibited from pastoral ministry. While I see the contradiction to the truth concerning Christ and His church, I hold that divorce and remarriage are not the unforgiveable sins, and honest repentance can afford the man to remain in the pastoral ministry. While I do not think divorce and remarriage in and of themselves are sins, they are the consequences of sin. Adultery and abandonment are more the sins. Somewhere in these two is the idea of abuse. There is divorce as a legal disposition and there can be divorce as a matter of life abandonment, emotionally, mentally, spiritually, and physically. But you can separate without separating physically and legally. Not that there is no hope of resurrection, but death can take place in the marital person wherein resurrection of the marriage is difficult. I believe this the situation for marriages that should have never been. The marriage began on life-support.

Second, the bishop must be sober-minded. This speaks of soundness and balance in discernment. Not mentally all over the landscape. If he is unstable in his personal life, he will probably be unstable in the pastoral ministry. This perhaps is the reason he should not be a new convert (1 Timothy 3:6) or immature spiritually. Being a watchman of souls requires a sober mind unmixed in thought. The other title for pastor is elder denoting maturity in the faith. A well-disciplined man in his life and the life of the church he pastors. He must not be flippant about life, but laser focused on what is valuable in life from God's point of view—the Bible.

Third, the pastor must be hospitable, showing love to strangers. This is the graciousness of the pastor. For he with the rest of the believers were strangers, but Christ took us in. In smelling like the sheep, the pastor doesn't minister from long distance. Like the Good and Great Shepherd, the shepherd of Christ's church is touchable. The scattered saints would need this quality to have shown them.

Fourth, the pastor must be able to teach. Teaching is more applicable to the pastoral ministry than preaching. Paul said that Christ's gift to the church was "pastor and teacher" wrapped up in the same person (Ephesians 4:11). When the pastor is only the preacher, he is the evangelist instead of the equipper. Now, there should be teaching in preaching. Truth must be imparted to the saints for the sake of transformation. The kerygma, the proclamation of the gospel, is certainly necessary. Jesus came into His ministry preaching the Gospel of the kingdom of heaven, but He taught His disciples through parables. John MacArthur stated, "Some may wonder why Paul includes this qualification in the midst of a list of moral qualities. He does so because effective teaching is woven into the moral character of the teacher. What a man is cannot be divorced from what he says."[33] In teaching and preaching, there is demonstration as well as proclamation (James 3:1). This is why teachers will be judged more strictly because they must practice what they teach.

Fifth, the bishop must be a life under the control of the Spirit and not anything else (Ephesians 5:18). If he is to demonstrate being guided by the Spirit, he must not be under the influence of wine or drugs. He must be sober-minded and sober-influenced by the Holy Spirit. He leads by example (1 Peter 5:3). As shepherd, he takes the point, he takes the lead, being the first one to face the enemies. The enemies want him to be a contradiction to the flock, so that they will wander and scatter in faith and practice (see Hebrews 13:7; Jeremiah 23:1-4; Ezekiel 34:1-10).

Sixth, the pastor must not be pugnacious, a striker, a fighter. He must control his temper with grace. Godly anger has its place, but not anger in defense of himself (Ephesians 4:26). He fights the good fight of faith, but not the people whom he leads towards the image of Christ.

> *"The Lord's servant must not be quarrelsome but kind to everyone, able to teach, patiently enduring evil, correcting his opponents with gentleness. God may perhaps grant them repentance leading to a knowledge of the truth, and they may come to their senses and escape from the snare of the devil, after being captured by him to do his will"* (2 Timothy 2:24-26, ESV).

Seventh, the elder must not be contentious, rather uncontentious. This is more a spirit of stirring up trouble. The pastor's task of creating unity and harmony in the church depends much on his disposition as peacemaker. His personality cannot be one of troublemaker with a boiling rage within himself. To remember that the sheep are not his, but Christ's, should affect the pastor's demeanor.

Eighth, the shepherd must not love money. He cannot be effective if he is driven by money and the things that money acquires. This will render the shepherd as a hireling, a mercenary which is the motives of false teachers (see 1 Peter 5:2; 2 Peter 2:1-3, 14). They must work for the glory of God and not for gold. They should not be muzzled but live by the support of the church (see 1 Timothy 5:17-18; 1 Corinthians 9:14) in accordance with the church's ability. Both the pastor and the people are to live by faith when it comes to pastor's financial needs. The pastor ought not to be greedy, and the people ought not to be stingy.

The prosperity movement in church could be driven by the love of money. Pastors who are bent in that direction desire to become the model of prosperity by promoting the members to seek wealth. Paul warns Timothy of the desire for riches:

> *"They that will be rich fall into temptation and a snare, and into many foolish and hurtful lusts, which drown men in destruction and perdition"* (1 Timothy 6:9, KJV).

It is not a sin to be rich nor is it godly to be poor. Although, God is concerned for the poor. They are not automatically children of God because of their poverty.

> *"It is easier for a camel to go through the eye of a needle, than for a rich man to enter into the kingdom of God"* (Mark 10:25, NKJV).

It is not *impossible* for the rich to enter into the kingdom of God, but it is dangerous to depend on your riches and not see that you are spiritually poor. The same is true of religious people who rest in their self-righteousness (Mark 10:17-27). It is okay to be rich and not commendable to be poor.

> *"The love of money is a root of all kinds of evils. It is through this craving that some have wandered away from the faith and pierced themselves with many pangs"* (1 Timothy 6:10, ESV).

The pastor must not himself focus on getting rich, nor lead the congregation to focus on getting rich. Being good stewards of God's resources can lead to being comprehensively rich (1 Timothy 6:6).

> *"Remove far from me vanity and lies: give me neither poverty nor riches; feed me with food convenient for me: Lest I be full, and deny thee, and say, who is the LORD? Or lest I be poor, and steal, and take the name of my God in vain"* (Proverbs 30:8-9, KJV).

The pastor who is greedy and loves money will misdirect the congregation towards the temporal at the expense of the eternal (1 Timothy 6:17-19).

> *"Do not lay up for yourselves treasures on earth, where moth and rust destroy and where thieves break in and steal, but lay up for yourselves treasures in heaven, where neither moth nor rust destroys*

and where thieves do not break in and steal. For where your treasure is, there your heart will be also" (Matthew 6:19-21, ESV).

Ninth, the pastor's home life is just as important and perhaps more important than his moral life. What he is at home is probably closer to who he really is. While he is at church, his actions can be professional performance. Almost every pastor has two churches. His home should be his miniature church that is foundational to the church he pastors. There should be a correlation between the two churches. If the miniature church is dysfunctional, the local congregation will be gravely affected. How the pastor presides over the primary church will determine how he presides over the secondary church. The pastor is called to manage both churches well, and the primary is crucial to the well-being of the local congregation. The pastor and his marriage and family should be a model for every marriage and family that comprises the local church. As bishop of family elders—heads of families, the overseer is responsible for demonstrating what it means to make, mark, mature, and multiply disciples. Healthy churches come out of healthy families, and the bishop's family is called to be an example of health. We are not talking about perfection but pursuing the kingdom of God and His righteousness manifested in the home. According, to the apostle Paul, disqualification sets in when there is marriage and family failure. If the bishop *"does not know how to manage his own household, how will he care for God's church?"* (1 Timothy 3:5, ESV).

It is most important that the wife and children of the pastor do not see a dichotomy between home life and church life. The pastor must not be a contradiction at home of who he purports to be at church. To a degree, the bishop's family is on display for modeling purposes. The children ought not to disgrace grace extended to them in salvation and sanctification. As the calling is high for the bishop, so the belonging to his family calls for obedience to his leadership towards the image of Jesus

Christ. They may not like that fact that they are on display, but it is a fact. This is why Christianity must be more than religious performance. It must be a relational response to the God who loved us in Christ Jesus. The wife and children must see a husband and father who is not religious, nor does he insist that they be religious with a whole lot of dos and don'ts, but a loving response to God. This is strengthened in children when it is obvious that their father loves Jesus, loves their mother, and loves them unconditionally. He must be a husband and father that is driven by grace and not law. The atmosphere in the pastor's home must not be legalistic but contagiously Christ-centered with a relational aroma.

> *"Hear, O Israel: The LORD our God, the LORD is one. You shall love the LORD your God with all your heart and with all your soul and with all your might. And these words that I command you today shall be on your heart. You shall teach them diligently to your children and shall talk of them when you sit in your house, and when you walk by the way, and when you lie down, and when you rise"* (Deuteronomy 6:4-7, ESV).

The bishop must not allow the church he pastors to supplant his first church—his marriage and family. This is part of him listening and obeying Paul's words to the Ephesian elders, "P*ay careful attention to yourselves*" (Acts 20:28, ESV) and then the rest of the secondary church. He must pay attention to his home life for it can undo the effectiveness of his pastoral life. A major part of the pastoral ministry is modeling from the home life into the church life (1 Peter 5:3).

Tenth, the elders of the church are not only to be "sober-minded" but "servant-minded" in order to prevent being conceited. Paul was concerned that a new convert if called by a church to pastor could not handle the high calling of the bishopric. That he would think more highly of himself than he ought (Philippians 2:3). Paul warned the leaders in Philippi of this danger as well the elders here. There is a danger in the high calling that the novice may not be able to manage. I have seen this struggle with experienced pastors. Those blessed with learning, leadership skills, preaching giftedness and trappings of what we think of as success, and become conceited. Titles inside the glorious church can lead to conceit: doctor, senior pastor, lead pastor, executive pastor, bishop and now apostles can cause us to think more highly of ourselves than we should. How about "Servant Pastor"? As Christian leaders, we can become so unlike Christ Jesus.

> *"Who though he was in the form of God, did not count equality with God a thing to be grasped, but emptied himself, by taking the form of a servant, being born in the likeness of men. And being found in human form, he humbled himself by becoming obedient to the point of death, even death on a cross"* (Philippians 2:6-8, ESV).

> *"Just as the Son of Man did not come to be served, but to serve, and to give His life a ransom for many"* (Matthew 20:28, NKJV).

There is the constant danger while pastoring in the glorious church that we reach for titles instead of the towel.

> *"Jesus knowing that the Father had given all things into His hands, and that He had come from God and was going to God, rose from supper and laid aside His garments, took a towel and girded Himself. After that, He poured water into a basin and began to wash the disciples' feet, and to wipe them with the towel with which He was girded. Then He came to Simon Peter. And Peter said to Him, 'Lord, are You washing my feet?' Jesus answered and said to him, 'what I am doing you do not understand now, but you will know after this.' Peter said to Him, 'You shall never wash my feet!' Jesus answered him, 'If I do not wash you, you have no part with Me.' Simon Peter said to Him, 'Lord, not my feet only, but also my hands and my head!'"* (John 13:3-9, NKJV).

Dr. Sandy Ray, who pastored the prestigious Cornerstone Baptist Church in Brooklyn, New York, who now lives upstairs with Christ who is Head of His church, made this profound observation:

> *"Jesus was not embarrassed to be girded in a towel because he knew that he was the only one in the fellowship who was tall enough to take a towel. The disciples walked on tiptoes seeking high seats; the Master took a towel. Jesus knew who he was, and he did not need any external pomp or regalia to prove who he was. He could have had angels serve him. He knew that he was a king in exile."*[34]

Like the apostle Paul, I believe that everyone who pastors in the glorious church need a "thorn in the flesh." It is a gift of grace to help us manage effectively the role of pastor in the Lord's church. It is not a sin, but rather a reminder of our disabilities in the high calling of pastoring. So, the apostle Paul said:

> *"So, to keep me from becoming conceited because of the surpassing greatness of the revelations, a thorn was given me in the flesh, a messenger of Satan to harass me, to keep me from becoming conceited"* (2 Corinthians 12:7, ESV).

The thorn in the flesh was not a sin, but it was there to keep Paul from sinning. The holy God would not use a sin or sins, like pride, ego, and self-sufficiency, to give Himself glory. God used Satan to administer this pain unto Paul—similar to Job's situation (Job 1:8-12). Oh pastor, what is your "thorn in the flesh" that keeps you humble before the feet of Jesus? Yes! There is grace in glory. For God's grace will provide the strength we need in our weaknesses in order for glory to be shown through our disabilities.

The pastor must live in the spirit of John the Baptist, who was a forerunner of Jesus Christ, called to prepare the way of the Lord. This was the task of the prophet John and must remain the task of the preacher pastor to exalt the Christ by decreasing so that men can see Jesus through us in preaching and pastoring. To get off of center stage is the task of the preacher/pastor, so that Christ, the main Star might shine in the hearts of the people. We do not want to impress outsiders, those outside of the faith, but we do want to impart truth, by not being a contradiction in word and deed. John the Baptist said that, *"He (Jesus) must increase, but I (John) must decrease"* (John 3:30, ESV—personal emphasis).

We have been looking at the qualification of the pastor, elder, bishop, shepherd of the local congregation of the glorious church of Jesus Christ. These qualifications are qualities, character traits, and imperative marks of the pastor. His assistants, the deacons who serve him, are to have similar traits as underlings functioning under the bishops (1 Timothy 3:8-13). All subsequent church leaders of our day must have like in kind traits.

Pastoral disqualification can be permanent, temporary, or intermittent. There could be levels of disqualifications. The apostate teachers are permanently disqualified (see 1 Timothy 1:18-19; 2 Timothy 2:17-19). Judas would fit this category (John 17:12). The temporary disqualified could be the one mentioned in 1 Corinthians 5:1-2; 1 Timothy 5:19, 20; Galatians 6:1. This level calls for repentance. The gravity of the action will determine the process and the degree of repentance (see 2 Samuel 12:7-14; Psalm 51; Micah 7:8). This would probably fit Peter (see Luke 22:32, 54-62; John 21:15-17). Now the intermittent disqualified, who occasionally act non-pastoral in word and deed, after admitting their wrong, can redeem their pastoral quality by asking for forgiveness. Then the pastoral influence can be regained. The high calling demands these lofty qualifications. The bishop is a soul watcher, who is responsible for overseeing each member's journey towards the image of Jesus Christ.

"Let no one despise you for your youth, but set the believers an example in speech, in *conduct, in love, in faith, in purity"* *(1 Timothy 4:12, ESV).*

"Brothers, join in imitating me, and keep your eyes on those who walk according to the example you have in us" (Philippians 3:17, ESV).

"Be imitators of me, as I am of Christ" (1 Corinthians 11:1, ESV).

Chapter 10

The Breath

"The ghost in the glorious church"

"Behold, I send the Promise of My Father upon you; but tarry in the city of Jerusalem until you are endued with power from on high."—Luke 24:49, NKJV

> *"When He had said this, He breathed on them, and said to them, Receive the Holy Spirit."*—John 20:22, NKJV

> *"You shall receive power when the Holy Spirit has come upon you; and you shall be witnesses to Me in Jerusalem, and in all Judea and Samaria, and to the end of the earth."*—Acts 1:8, NKJV

The breath of the glorious church is the presence and power of the Holy Spirit. As in the beginning of creation the Holy Spirit is present in creative power lingering over the face of the waters (Genesis 1:1.2), so is the Spirit crucial to the life of the church and her members. The human life is of the Spirit: *"Then the LORD God formed man of the dust from the ground and breathed into his nostrils the breath of life, and the man became a living creation"* (Genesis 2:7, ESV).

The new man, as the church, is a living organism because of the breath of the Spirit. The physical and the spiritual realities are the product of the Spirit. Moreover, the Spirit is vital and viable to the visible church, the manifestation of the invisible church on earth. We have spoken of **Him**, <u>not</u> **it**, previously as operative in regeneration.

> *Jesus answered, "Most assuredly, I say to you, unless one is born of water and the Spirit, he cannot enter the kingdom of God. That which is born of the flesh is flesh, and that which is born of the Spirit is spirit. Do not marvel that I said to you, 'you must be born again.' The wind blows where it wishes, and you hear the sound of it, but cannot tell where it comes from and where it goes. So is everyone who is born of the Spirit"* (John 3:5-8, NKJV).

We have also spoken of the Spirit as operative in the forming of the church, the second body of Christ on earth.

> *"As the body is one and has many members, but all the members of that one body, being many, are one body, so also is Christ. For by one Spirit, we were all baptized into one body—whether Jews or Greeks, whether slaves or free—and have all been made to drink into one Spirit. For in fact the body is not one member but many"* (1 Corinthians 12:12-14, NKJV).

In this chapter, the focus is on the power of the Spirit in the life and ministry of the church and Christian. The disobedient church in fulfilling the Master's Mandate—making, marking, maturing, and multiplying disciples—is found in the Spirit being inoperative in the church. This is the dispensation of the Spirit but the church functions as if there was no Spirit. His advent was specifically into the Christian and church, but He seems to be the neglected Spirit and the unknown Spirit. We can understand the ignorance of John the Baptist's disciples for they had not come to Jesus at that time (Acts 19:1-7), but the Holy Spirit has birthed, baptized and indwelled the believer and He is inoperative in the life of the church and Christian. This is sad and shameful to announce this condition in today's Christian church. It looks as if the church has relegated Him either to an emotional experience or to the baptism and benedictory ceremonies. The Spirit is the best player on the team, and He is riding the bench in the game of life and the great ministry of the church. No wonder He weeps (Ephesians 4:30). He is the gift to the church and Christian and He is neglected and ignored. The impotence of the Christian and church is certainly found in the Spirit being inoperative. The inexplicable is not happening for there are no signs of the performance enhancing presence and power of the Spirit. The Christian church operates as a mere organization and not an organism because the church is operating in the natural and not the supernatural. She is ordinary and not extraordinary, for the Spirit is grieving because we won't let Him take over the operations of the church, moving the church beyond organization to functioning as an organism. The dynamic of the church has been drained out by tradition, bylaws, constitutions, programs, ritualism, secularism, socialism, religiosity, and non-spiritual agendas. The Holy Spirit will not participate in our churches, only in Christ's church. Many churches have organized in the name of Christ, but function in their own names. The Spirit will participate only in churches that glorify Jesus Christ and His purpose for His church (see Matthew 16:13-20; 28:19, 20; John 16:5-15). The visible church is glorious when she is "Ghost up"—that is, filled, and blown along by the Holy Ghost.

The command is not to be baptized or indwelled by the Spirit but to be filled—blown along by the Spirit. The baptism and the indwelling are in the indicative, the case of reality, but to be filled is in the present, imperative tense of the continuous need of the filling of the Spirit. This filling is not stagnant rather dynamic as the wind filling the sail moving the ship through the sea to its destination and designed purpose.

The Holy Spirit is the gift to the Christian and church. He is Promised Power. His coming to empower the Christian and the church was not conditional. Jesus promised that the Father would send the power. In John 14:16, Jesus said, *"And I will pray the Father and He shall give you another Comforter, that He may abide with you forever."* The Holy Spirit was the gift from God to Jesus' disciples and every believer. They did not have to merit the Spirit's coming, but only wait for His arrival. In Luke 24:49, Jesus stated that He would send the promise of His Father upon them, so they were instructed to wait until they were endued with power. Sense God exists in a holy society, it makes no difference who sends the Spirit, whether the Father or the Son, for they are one.

The purpose of the Christian church could not be effectively accomplished without the promised power of the Spirit. The church's purpose to reach the whole world with the Gospel of grace was too great for these ordinary men and women to reach without the performance enhancing promised power of the Spirit.

> *"This is the word of the* Lord *to Zerubbabel: 'Not by might, nor by power, but by my Spirit, says the* Lord *of hosts"* (Zechariah 4:6, ESV).

Jesus promised them that they would do greater things than He had done, but actually the Holy Spirit would do the greater things through them. We know that the work of Christ on earth is matchless and that He is the peerless Christ, but the expansion of the work would be greater, reconciling the whole world to God in Christ through His church mammoth endeavor. Evangelizing the world with the Gospel of grace through the strategy of making, marking, maturing and multiplying disciples is doing greater things. In the book of Acts, we fundamentally have the acts of the Holy Spirit through the apostles, and the visible church of Jesus Christ.

It is necessary for us to understand that the book of Acts is the historical narrative of the advent of the Holy Spirit and the birth of the church and the development of this infant assembly of believers. We must not form theological constructs during these developmental stages of the church. Holy Spirit's coming was not conditioned on them being on one accord. The coming of the Holy Spirit on the Day of Pentecost was a historic event not to be repeated nor to usher in the thought of the need for a second blessing of the Holy Spirit after salvation. There are no instructions by the apostles for believers to seek the baptism or the indwelling of the Holy Spirit. After Pentecost, Samaria and Caesarea Philippi, the Holy Spirit was (and is) the gift in salvation to all believers. One does not need to tarry for the Holy Spirit, He is the promised gift to the believer and church. The promise of the Spirit is not to some elite Christians or the mature Christians, but for all believers.

> *"On the last day of the feast, the great day, Jesus stood up and cried out, 'if anyone thirsts, let him come to me and drink. Whoever believes in me, as the Scripture has said, out of his heart will flow rivers of living water.' Now this he said about the Spirit, whom those who believed in him were to receive, for as yet the Spirit had not been given, because Jesus was not yet glorified"* (John 7:37-39, ESV).

> *"By one Spirit we were all baptized into one body—whether Jews or Greeks, whether slaves or free—and have all been made to drink into the one Spirit"* (1 Corinthians 12:13, NKJV).

> *"You are not in the flesh but in the Spirit, if indeed the Spirit of God dwells in you. Now if anyone does not have the Spirit of Christ, he is not His"* (Romans 8:9, NKJV).

All believers have the gift of the Holy Spirit, without exceptions. There is no salvation and no relationship with the Father and Son without the presence of the Holy Spirit. He is promised power in every believer.

It is very important that we get our minds around the truth that the Holy Spirit is Personage Power. The Spirit is a person without physiology. He is not an impersonal force. He is not mere power or energy. He is person, just like the Father and the Son, who became man in time but in eternity He was without flesh (John 1, 14). The Holy Spirit is referred to in terms that denote personhood. In the Great Commission passage, we see His equality with the First Person and Second Person of the Trinity (Matthew 28:19-20). If they are Persons, so is He. He is a distinct Person in the mystery of plural oneness. He is not some impersonal force of the Father or the Son. Omnipotence is the natural attribute of each member of the holy society, called the Trinity. As Person, He has feelings (Ephesians 4:30). As Person, He can be lied to (Acts 5:3). As Person, He can comfort just as Jesus is our comforter (John 14:16). As Person, He has understanding and wisdom (1 Corinthians 2:10-11). Impersonal force does not have wisdom and understanding. As Person, He has will (1 Corinthians 12:11). As Person, He loves (Romans 15:30). As Person, He can speak and teach (see 1 Timothy 4:1; Revelation 2:7; John 14:26). As Person, He has authority (Acts 13:2) and can intercede for us (Romans 8:26). Jesus Christ announced the personhood of the Spirit when He said, *"Nevertheless I tell you the truth. It is to your advantage that I go away; for if I do not go away, the Helper will not come to you; but if I depart, I will send Him to you"* (John 16:7). Jesus definitely refers to the personhood of the Spirit.

We dare not miss the personhood of the Spirit in His relationship language with the Father and the Son because of His subordination to them. He is known as the Spirit of God and the Spirit of Christ. This is not modalism wherein the One God is acting out the roles of Father, Son and Holy Spirit. It is the mystery of the intra-Trinitarians God. Although, there is distinction in the plural oneness, there in unity in the functioning. So, we can say the Spirit of God and the Spirit of Christ without removing the Holy Spirit as the Third Person of the Godhead. He can be the Spirit of God and of Christ and yet be Himself in the holy society.

> *"When He had been baptized, Jesus came up immediately from the water; and behold, the heavens were opened to Him, and He saw the Spirit of God descending like a dove and alighting upon*

> *Him. And suddenly a voice came from heaven, saying, 'this is My beloved Son, in whom I am well pleased'"* (Matthews 3:16-17, NKJV).

> *"The grace of the Lord Jesus Christ, and love of God, and the communion of the Holy Spirit be with you all. Amen"* (2 Corinthians 13:14, NKJV).

> *"God was manifested in the flesh, Justified in the Spirit, Seen by angels, Preached among the Gentiles, Believed on in the world, Received up in glory"* (1 Timothy 3:16, NKJV).

In that the Holy Spirit is personage power tells us that He does not give us power. He does not *have* power, He *is* power. To have power is to be indwelled by Him who is power; the power that we are given to do the work of God. The disciples of Jesus were waiting on the Holy Spirit in order to be Christ's witnesses and that power was in the person of the Holy Spirit. To say we need power to preach, serve, witness, love, etc., is really saying we need the Holy Spirit to be operative in our lives. He does not give us power on loan, but the gift of the Spirit is Himself the power within us.

> *"You shall receive power when the Holy Spirit is come upon you; and shall be witnesses to Me in Jerusalem, and in all Judea and Samaria, and to the end of the earth"* (Acts 1:8, NKJV).

In actuality, Jesus promised that the Spirit would not merely be upon them but in them.

> *"If you love Me, keep My commandments. And I will pray the Father, and He will give you another Helper, that He may abide with you forever—the Spirit of truth, whom the world cannot receive, because it neither sees Him nor knows Him; but you know Him, for He dwells with you and will be in you"* (John 14:15-17, NKJV).

It appears that the Spirit's operation is from the inside of the believer and not an anointment power. The coming upon is probably the advent, the coming down into the believer. As Jesus made His advent through the Virgin Mary into the world, so the Spirit made His advent through the believer into the world. The Holy Spirit, as Breath, denotes inward presence, and, as Wind, outward force moving the sailboat along to its destination and purpose. But the major point here is that the Spirit is personage power. Like God is love, so God is power. When God is in you there is love and there is power. The Spirit does not place power into our hands, rather He places us into the Hands of Power. We must not let the metaphoric terms like "wind, water, power, ghost, spirit and breath" cause us to think in impersonal terms concerning the Holy Spirit. These terms must be understood in the light of the context wherein they are found, but in most cases, they are descriptive of the effects of this Powerful Person in the life of the believer and church.

The Holy Spirit is Permanent Power. He comes to dwell in the believer forever. The Spirit has always been present in His world for He is omnipresent just as the Father, who is Spirit is everywhere at the same time. In the is-ness of God there is also the everywhere-ness of God. There is no past tense nor future tense in His existence, only the present tense. We often speak of God in anthropomorphic terms like "God came down," "God came seeking," and "God appeared" to denote Him taking the initiatives into the world's events and human situation, but God does not need to travel for He exists in the eternal here. If there is anywhere, He will not be, it is hell.

But the gloriousness of the Christian and church of Jesus Christ is the specificity of the Holy Spirit's presence in the life of the Christian and church. Like Mary was highly favored, so is the Christian and church highly favored. The Word that was with God in the beginning became flesh through the Virgin Mary, entering the world. And now the Spirit who was also with God in the beginning comes to operate exclusively through the Christian and church. His presence is a permanent presence, not intermittent as with the Old Testament saints (see Judges 14:6; Ezekiel 2:2; Psalm 51:11). In the new dispensation of the Spirit, He will remain forever. He may weep, but He will not leave us (Ephesians 4:30).

The Holy Spirit is Purposeful Power and essentially He is the Spirit of truth, in that, He enables the believer and the church to tell the truth about Jesus Christ, who is the Truth. Jesus is the incarnate truth for He is the self-disclosure of God the Father, and He also is the Truth about authentic humanity. The Holy Spirit is the internal truth resident in the believer and church enabling us to tell the truth about Jesus Christ, the God-Man.

> *"In the beginning was the Word (the Son of God), and the Word was with God (co-equal), and the Word was God (continuously). . . . And the Word became flesh (man) and dwelt among us (social), and we have seen his glory, glory as of the only Son from the Father, full of grace and truth"* (John 1:1,14, ESV—personal emphasis).

> *"Jesus said to him, 'I am the way and the truth, and the life. No one comes to the Father except through me. If you had known me, you would have known my Father also. From now on you do know him and have seen him.' Philip said to him, 'Lord, show us the Father.' Whoever has seen me has seen the Father. How can you say, show us the Father'? Do you not believe that I am in the Father and the Father is in me? The words that I say to you I do not speak on my own authority, but the Father who dwells in me does his works. Believe me that I am in the Father and the Father is in me, or else believe on account of the works themselves"* (John 14:6-11, ESV).

Also, when the Spirit of Truth has come to operate exclusively in the Christian and church, He will confront the world of their need of salvation, but this will not be done apart from the Christian and church. Remember, His work in the world is through the Christian church, which is why the visible church is glorious as salt and light in the world. The Spirit has come to function inside of the confines of the body of Christ. This is what He will do:

> *"He will convict the world concerning sin and righteousness and judgment, concerning sin, because they do not believe in me; concerning righteousness, because I go to the Father, and you will see me no longer, concerning judgment, because the ruler of this world is judged"* (John 16:8-11, ESV).

The believer in their believing will be used of the Holy Spirit in convicting the world of the root sin of unbelief. The believer in right relationship with God will be used of the Holy Spirit to convict the world of unrighteousness, and Christ's position at the right hand of the throne of God testifies to our standing in righteousness. The believer's standing in justification is evidence that Satan, the prince of this world, was judged and defeated on the Cross of Calvary, and thus the whole world is under judgment (see 1 John 5:19; Colossians 2:15; John 12:31). Dr. Wiersbe states:

> *"It is important to note that the Spirit comes to the church and not the world. This means that He works in and through the church. The Holy Spirit does not minister in a vacuum. Just as the Son of God had to have a body in order to do His work on earth, so the Spirit of God needs a body to accomplish His ministries; and the body is the church. Our bodies are His tools and temples, and He wants to use us to glorify Christ and to witness to a lost world."*[35]

> *"There can be no conversion without conviction, and there can be no conviction apart from the Spirit of God using the Word of God and the witness of the child of God."*[36]

The purpose of the Spirit mainly is to enable the saints for the work of the ministry. He is the gift to the Christian and church. He regenerates, quickens, enlightens, teaches, guides, inspires, intercedes, comforts, seals, cleanses, gives gifts, and more for the sake of reaching the world with the Gospel of grace. This is the dispensation of the Holy Spirit and Christ's church.

The Holy Spirit is Particular Power. He operates exclusively in and through members of the body of Christ. His advent into the world is really His taking up residence in the believers who belong to the body of Christ. When Jesus promised in Matthew 28:20 that He would be with His disciples and with us forever, He probably had in mind the Holy Spirit, the other comforter (John 14:16-18). We have also spoken of the temple presence of the Holy Spirit in the believer and in the church (1 Corinthians 6:19; 3:16-17). These are the particular dwellings of the Spirit. What a glorious privilege and responsibility for believers to be sanctuaries of the Spirit's operations in the world. The power is not necessarily for our benefit rather to enable us through gifting to bring glory to Christ through us for the sake of the redemption of the world.

Parenthetically, let me discuss the Paradox of Power. Power in the powerless for God's glory. Jesus promised that the Holy Spirit, the powerful Person would reside in the weak believers and church (see John 7:37-39; 14:17; Luke 24:49; Acts 1:5-8). The Holy Spirit would enable the natural to become supernatural, the ordinary to become extra-ordinary. In actuality, God does not want us strong but weak. What a paradox! God does not want us working for Him, rather He wants to work through us. In the Old Testament, Israel is often placed in impossible situations in order for God to get the glory. God is constantly disciplining Israel's faith and challenging them to depend upon Him. God's discipline was often due to their disobedience, but through it all, they were constantly discovering their weakness and at times their wickedness as the covenant people of God.

The Christian witness is perfected in weakness. Paul made this profound and paradoxical discovery *"that God's power was made perfect in weakness"* (2 Corinthians 12:9). This is antithetical to the world's thinking, but it is necessary for achieving *Soli Deo Gloria*—for God's glory alone. The transcended purpose of the church's existence in the world demands the inexplicable be done for God to receive the glory. A world captured by the idolatry of humanism knows nothing of celebrating weakness in order for God getting what is due Him. It is not an accident that Christ chose ordinary men to do extraordinary things. Peter and the rest of the disciples were weak men but through the Spirit, especially after Pentecost, they were enabled to begin Christ's worldwide vision to reach the entire world with the Gospel of grace. This was the reason they were told to wait on the advent of the Spirit. For without the Spirit, they would be disadvantaged and disabled on their own to accomplish the great mission of the glorious church. Salvation commences in weakness: *"Blessed are the poor in spirit"* (Matthew 5:3); and, in sanctification and service, Christians and the church need to continue in their weakness (Philippians 2:12-13).

Our salvation was obtained by God becoming weak. Wow! We see this in Jesus Christ, the Son of God, being humiliated to gain our redemption (Philippians 2:5-11). It wasn't the strong Jesus, but the weak Jesus that secured human salvation (2 Corinthians 8:9). It wasn't the sovereign, but the Savior, it wasn't the Creator God, but the crucified God; it wasn't the Lion of the tribe of Judah, but the Lamb slain before the foundation of the world; it wasn't the king, but the kinsman redeemer; it wasn't the Rose of Sharon, but the root out of dry ground; it wasn't He who was rich, but He who became poor; it wasn't the healer, but the wounded; it wasn't the Prince of Peace, but He who became the propitiation of our sins. Listen: *"For He was crucified in weakness but lives by the power of God. For we also are weak in him, but in dealing with you, we will live with Him by the power of God"* (2 Corinthians 13:4, ESV).

Without the breath of the Holy Spirit, the Christian and the church are the walking dead. We are like Ezekiel's bones—formed, but lifeless. We are organized, but not functioning as an organism. We are having church, but not being the church. There is structure and style void of the performance enhancing Spirit. The ineffectiveness of the Christian church makes obvious that the church is not on Spirit performance enhancing power, making the church exceptional in the world. "*Can these bones live?*" (Ezekiel 37:3, ESV).

The prognosticators of the church have almost written the church off. They are writing on the autopsy of the church of Jesus Christ, while she still lives, to see why she is dying. What is causing her decline and ensuing death? Young adults are no longer interested in attending the church. People are discussing whether or not the church is still relevant, and whether Christianity needs to widen its reach in some form of universalism to survive in a pluralistic age. Some Christians and churches are feeling desperate, closing their doors and merging (which may not be a bad idea). But other congregations are looking for new techniques and strategies to keep from dying or becoming irrelevant. "Can these bones live?" Many are not saying "*Lord, you know whether or not life can enter these dry and dead bones*" (Ezekiel 37:3—paraphrased). They are just ready to give the benediction over the church and seek some alternate solutions to the social ills.

Have we forgotten that it is Christ's church, and He said He would build it and death will not prevail or be the end to His church? The living Head and the living body is indispensable. There will be no divorce or destruction of the church of Jesus Christ. Because He lives, the church will remain until she is raptured to her Lord in the air (1 Thessalonians 4:17).

The Lord told Ezekiel, as worker, that the word and the Wind is the answer to the dry, divided, and dead condition of the bones. The church today needs unashamed workers rightly dividing the Word of Truth to bring a divided church together in order that the Wind—the Spirit—can revive the bones to become a militant force in the world (see Ezekiel 37:1-10; 2 Timothy 2:14-15).

The Biography

The Author's Journey

"Before I formed you in the womb, I knew you, and before you were born, I consecrated you; I appointed you a prophet to the nations."—Jeremiah 1:5, ESV

My journey with the Lord started in eternity. In the mind of the omniscient God, I was purposed to preach and to shepherd His people. It was predetermined in eternity that I would become a preacher of the Gospel of grace, and then a pastor of God's people. It was not a professional quest or decision of mine, but the quickening and urging of the Spirit of God. Like the prophet Jeremiah, my calling was a Divine setup from eternity.

As far as I can remember, I was acquainted with God. However, I did not personally know Him, nor did I have a relationship with His Son Jesus Christ. Before the term *easy believism* was used to identify a mere Christian, I was a victim of having a knowledge of God and Jesus Christ but void of having a personal commitment to Him. The awareness of the Gospel and my need to respond to it was somewhat lost in my first church experience. But thank God for a praying mother who was led by the Holy Spirit to move my brother and me to a place (Lake Elsinore, California) where we could encounter God in Christ beyond intellectual assent to having a personal relationship with Him.

My salvation experience was not marked by a definitive event in history. I did not have a Pauline experience of salvation. It did not occur on some Damascus Road, in some dramatic fashion. I did not see, hear, nor feel something strange and mysterious. I cannot date my salvation inception any more than I can date my physical inception. However, both are evidential in birth and being. The result of inception is the most important evidence of new life in Christ. It is the life of the believer that marks that there was inception and birth. When we take notice of the other apostles of Jesus, there were no dramatic events that marked their salvation, either. There was just a response to Jesus' call to follow Him. Many people followed Jesus, but as fans, rather than authentic followers of Christ. Evidently, something happened in the authentic followers that did not take place in the mere followers of Jesus. The evidence of salvation is certainly more important than the event of salvation; however, evidence of the new life in Christ will manifest itself in time. One can point to a time, but is there evidence of a transformation? For me the birthday is not remembered, but the evidence of new life in Christ is. In time I discovered that I was saved, I had moved from intellectual assent to an authentic faith and an authentic relationship with Christ.

> *"Truly, truly, I say to you, whoever hears my word and believes him who sent me has eternal life. He does not come into judgment but has passed from death to life"* (John 5:24, ESV).

> *"This is the testimony that God gave us eternal life, and this life is in his Son. Whoever has the Son has life; whoever does not have the Son of God does not have life"* (1 John 5:11-12, ESV).

> *"No one born of God makes a practice of sinning, for God's seed abides in him; and he cannot keep on sinning, because he has been born of God. By this it is evident who the children of God are, and who are the children of the devil; whoever does not practice righteousness is not of God, nor is the one who does not love his brother"* (1 John 3:9-10, ESV).

While I was predetermined to become Jesus' workmanship, I was also predetermined to become His worker.

> *"We are His workmanship, created in Christ Jesus for good works, which God prepared beforehand that we should walk in them"* (Ephesians 2:10, NKJV).

> *"Be diligent to present yourself approved of God, a worker who does not need to be ashamed, rightly dividing the word of truth"* (2 Timothy 2:15, NKJV).

I am the product of this mysterious call to preach the Gospel of Jesus Christ. You hear this mystery in the Lord's response to Ananias who hesitated to go and minister to Saul of Tarsus after Saul's encounter with the Lord Jesus on the Road to Damascus. Listen to what the Lord said to Him:

> *"Go, for he (Saul) is a chosen instrument of mine to carry my name before kings and the children of Israel. For I will show him how much he must suffer for the sake of my name"* (Acts 9:15-16, ESV).

As my salvation and call to preach was predetermined by God, so this matter of pastoring was divine in origin. It was a desire (1 Timothy 3:1), but where the desire originated makes it more divine than human. It was a God thing. The weight of the matter of pastoring had to be realized in time. I must admit that there were some superficialities in my desire to pastor. When I got through the seemly privileges of being a bishop and realized that the role of the bishop was primarily to oversee the members' journey towards the image of Jesus Christ, and that I must give an account of my shepherding to the Chief Shepherd, holy fear gripped me then and even to this day, it causes me to tremble. The character qualifications of the pastor led me to understand my role as an example to the flock in pursuance of becoming more like Jesus Christ. Yes, leadership is influence, but towards the image of Jesus Christ more than anything else.

It was not just leading the members to do, but to become. Charisma and credentials have their places, but character is most essential to leadership. This sobered me greatly and has revolutionized my role and function as shepherd living among the sheep and smelling like the sheep, but in front of the sheep as model. The destination of the leader who leads is towards Christlikeness. This is what Paul meant when he said:

> *"My little children, for whom I labor in birth again until Christ is formed in you"* (Galatians 4:19, NKJV).

If this is not sobering enough, the Hebrew writer declared that the pastor is a soul watcher. He is not merely a watcher of the silver, service, sanctuary, Scriptures, structure, sacraments, speaking, and staff, but moreover, souls. He is entrusted with souls. He watches over that which is eternal. The body does not go into eternity until it is changed, but the soul goes immediately into the presence of God. The work of all the professions in life (politicians, philosophers, scientists, anthropologists, sociologists, attorneys, judges, police officers, physicians, geologists, religionists, psychologists, astronauts and others) ends at the grave, but the pastor's work ends in eternity. Only the soul goes into the presence of the Lord, in peace or in judgment. The soul, the immaterial, intangible self, the real you, goes into eternity. The pastor is responsible for that person's growth and maturity towards the image of Jesus Christ. This is man's returning to his oughtness in Christ. Marred in the first Adam, restored in the second Adam, Jesus Christ (Romans 3:23; 1 John 3:1-3). The profundity of the pastor's role causes me to ask, who would desire to be a bishop? For it is an awesome task. I entered the pastorate not fully grasping the depth of it all. Even after fifty-four years, I still tremble at the high calling of pastoring the people of God. I am a caretaker of the second body of Christ on earth. The older I get, the more I pastor with a godly fear. To know that I have been entrusted with souls, members of the glorious body of Christ, the Bride of Christ, is overwhelming to say the least. Souls are precious to the Lord. Souls are the essence of humanity. For God created us as living souls (Genesis 2:7). We are God's value in dust. And Jesus asked the rhetorical questions:

> *"What does it profit a man to gain the whole world and forfeit his soul? For what can a man give in return for his soul?"* (Mark 8:36-37, ESV).

I have pastored two churches in the last fifty-four years—ten years as pastor of the Shiloh Baptist Church in Banning, California, and over forty-four years as pastor of the Mt. Zion Baptist Church in Redwood City, California. In my first privilege of pastor, I grew up from being an emotive preacher to preaching and pastoring that focused more on life transformation. While never being ashamed of my emotions, I did not focus there. I was taught to be doctrinal in my preaching as a young preacher, but these later years I am still doctrinal in my preaching and teaching but more with a bent towards incarnational growth of the hearer and doer of the word. My preaching and teaching motive has changed over the years. My preaching/teaching ministry has morphed into purposeful expositional kerygma to affect change in the life of the people. I have developed the desire for the congregation to know, to do and become. I want them to know the Gospel, to become a Gospel, and to share the Gospel—music first and then lyrics. Years ago, I grew out of preaching for self-validation to desiring to edify the saints for the work of the ministry. However, there is still the struggle at times to decrease that Christ might increase (John 3:30). There is the constant danger in preaching, for me, to be at the center, while on center stage. Jesus is the Star; I am just a supporting cast. I often wonder, after preaching, who is on the minds of the people—Jesus or the preacher. Do the hearers leave worship saying, "Oh, how wonderful Jesus is!" Or "Pastor Campbell—what a great preacher he is!" It is my heart's desire that when the preaching is done, Christ is exulted, and the hearers are raptured in the greatness of our God and Christ. I am constantly aware of Paul's words:

"We have this treasure in earthen vessels that the excellence of the power may be of God and not of us" (2 Corinthians 4:7, NKJV).

What also grips me as pastor is Paul's words to the Elders as he admonishes them: "*Therefore take heed to yourselves and to all the flock, among which the Holy Spirit has made them overseers, to shepherd the church of God which He purchased with His own blood*" (Acts 20:28, NKJV).

This passage leads me to constantly ask myself, 'what are my motives in preaching and pastoring the church that belongs to Him, that He has died she might exist?' The glorious church demands a crucified preacher and pastor in order that the resurrected Christ is the preeminent Person in the life of His church.

The Epilogue

The Bonus

"An identifiable pattern of the church"

Without fear of contradiction this is a problematic age in which we now live. However, this is not new, for every age has been problem-ridden. Ever since the fall of man, our world has been plagued with problems. We have become more civilized and more corrupted at the same time. Dr. S. M. Lockridge well said the following: "This is an age of guided missiles and misguided men."[37] Social evolution is more devolution. Morally, ethically, relationally, and spiritually, man is moving away from the God of objective truth. The prophet Isaiah has said of his age that, *"Justice is turned back, and righteousness stands far away; for truth has stumbled in the public squares, and uprightness cannot enter. Truth is lacking, and he who departs from evil makes himself a prey"* (Isaiah 59:14-15, ESV). The subjective god, created by man and for man rejects objective truth of the living God. This man-made god and his worshippers believe in situational ethics, political correctness, and undisciplined and ungodly democracy. The apostle Paul forecasted and chronicled our day when he wrote:

> "Understand this, that in the last days there will come times of difficulty. For people will be lovers of self, lovers of money, proud, arrogant, abusive, disobedient to their parents, ungrateful, unholy, heartless, unappeasable, slanderous, without self-control, brutal, not loving good, treacherous, reckless, swollen with conceit, lovers

of pleasures rather than lovers of God, having the appearance of godliness, but denying its power. Avoid such people" (2 Timothy 3:1-5, ESV).

Dr. Lloyd C. Blue suggested that the problems of this world in part can be attributed to the church in disobedience to the Great Commandment and Commission. In a sermon entitled "Why the Storm?" Dr. Blue used the life and ministry of the prophet Jonah as a model of the church in disobedience. The condition of the world might be partly the results of the church being off mission and purpose. This runaway prophet is an identifiable pattern of the church. Where is the salty church holding back the moral rottenness? Where is the lighthouse church illuminating the truth of God in a dark world? Where is the church the colony of the kingdom of God, living otherworldly in this world? Where is the church the ambassadors for Christ in a foreign world? Where is the reconciled community in a world gone astray from God? When we miss our purpose for being in the world, we cause problems in the world, for there is not a replacement for the church. We exclusively are the salt and light in the earth and world. God has no plan "B." The church is it—the community of hope in a hopeless world.

The Church in Defiance

> *"The word of the* LORD *came to Jonah the son of Amittai, saying, 'Arise, go to Nineveh, the great city, and cry out against it, because their wickedness has come up before Me.' But Jonah got up to flee to Tarshish from the presence of the* LORD. *So he went down to Joppa, found a ship that was going to Tarshish, paid the fare, and boarded it to go with them to Tarshish away from the presence of the* LORD.*"*—Jonah 1:1-3, NASB

Jonah rebelled against the Word of God which in essence is rebelling against God. The strategy of the enemy is always for us to go against what God has said. That was Adam and Eve's problem—they argued and went against the Word of God. To change or add to the Word of God is the same as going against His Word. The Bible is the foundation for the church and the believer. To deny its truth is to remove the foundation on which we stand as the people of God. As in Adam and Eve's situation, Satan wanted them to distrust and disobey the command of God, and for that, they went down and all of humanity went down with them. The best kind of church and Christian is an obedient church and Christian. If the Word of God is absent, the church is powerless and without direction. What we believe about God, creation, man, sin, salvation, and the future is found in Scripture. The Bible is under attack from within the church and from without the church. From the secular world to the Jesus Seminar so-called scholars, the Bible is rendered unreliable and irrelevant. As I have said, this is not new (Genesis 2:15-17; 3:1-7). Disobedience in man is as old as Adam and Eve.

It is amazing that one can believe in the existence of God who finds His existence in Himself and created the universe out of nothing and sustains it by His own power cannot inspire an inerrant book as it relates to the original manuscripts. To say that the miracles of the Bible are only myths is to make God into our own image of incapability. Why doubt the authenticity of the Bible? Because finite men cannot comprehend the infinite, incomprehensible God. The Bible is the Word of God. It is not given merely for our reading pleasure, but to help us to know God's will and to do His will. Therefore, the Word of God came to Jonah commanding him to go to Nineveh and cry out against it. It was a clear word from the Lord. It was not a user-friendly or non-offensive approach to preaching. Jonah was to cry out against the wickedness of the city, warning them to repent or suffer the consequences of their wickedness and sins. It was up to them. They could experience God's mercy or His wrath. Jonah, driven by his disdain for the Ninevites and his understanding of the mercy and grace of God, deliberately disobeyed the clear Word of the Lord (Jonah 4:2). Jonah did not change the message; he just wouldn't preach the message in fear that they just might repent. Jonah didn't want mercy, rather wrath. So, he decides not to evangelize the Ninevites with the Gospel of grace.

Jonah was guilty of disobeying God and going in the wrong direction from the will and work of God. He went, but not for God nor to where God told him to go. This is the state of some Christian churches today. They are busy doing and going in their own directions. Some are busy majoring in minors or engaging in partial obedience (1 Samuel 15:10-23). The Lord sent Jonah on a salvific mission and not a social ministry mission. As Jesus came seeking the lost for salvation, so must the church prioritize what He majored in (see Luke 19:10; 2 Corinthians 5:18-21). Everything else the church does must become ancillary to the Great Commission and this is truly obeying the Great Commandment (see Matthew 28:19-20; 22:38-40).

The "Jonah Baptist Church of Tarshish" is an example of the church going off course. It is the church going in the wrong direction from Christ's purpose for His church. It is supposed to be evangelizing in Nineveh, but it is engaged in a Tarshish agenda, conforming to the wishes of the world, who think they know what the church of Jesus Christ ought to be doing in the world. Jonah went with them to Tarshish. He followed the world instead of God. He chose his own assignment away from God's presence and purpose. The Tarshish church is the church that goes in the direction of the world. It is the church that majors in what Jesus minored in, and minors in what Jesus majored in. It is a church that majors in having church programs, events, fund raisers, building projects, social ministries, and pastor anniversaries. The Tarshish type churches are more concerned about counting people than weighing them. It is more concerned about numerical growth than incarnational growth. The Tarshish churches majors in helping people cope instead of leading them to change. The Tarshish churches are religious in nature more than relational.

The "Jonah Baptist Mega Church of Tarshish" can intimidate smaller congregations when this church appears to be the standard of success and effectiveness. Big, busy, buildings, budgets and broadcasting does not always spell obedience. Your church can be the "Jonah Baptist Church of Nineveh" no matter the size. Also, a smaller church can be a Tarshish church—it is all determined by obedience. Any church that is engaged in doing good things at the expense of the best thing is disobedient. The late pastor/preacher, Dr. Mack King Carter said in a sermon some years ago, "That if Jesus would return to earth and join one of our churches, He would have to go through new member's class, for He would not recognize His church." The church in defiance is the church going in the wrong direction. They have misunderstood or are just defiant and want church on their own terms, according to the felt needs of the people, not understanding that the root of every social ill is sin. Obeying the Great Commission, making, marking, maturing, and multiplying disciples is the answer to social ills when understood comprehensively.

The Church in Deep Sleep

> *"Then the sailors became afraid and every man cried out to his god, and they hurled the cargo which was in the ship into the sea to lighten it for them. But Jonah had gone below into the stern of the ship, had lain down, and fallen sound asleep. So the captain approached him and said, 'How is it that you are sleeping? Get up, call on your god! Perhaps your god will be concerned about us so that we will not perish.'"*—Jonah 1:5-6, NASB

Jonah was fast asleep in the lower part of a ship that was in the midst of a storm with lives in jeopardy. He was sound asleep, unconscious of the impending danger. This is an identifiable pattern of some churches, asleep in the midst of a storm. The word *sleep* is used metaphorically for being 'unaware.' Not aware of what's going on around them—ignorant of the times, thus doing ministry as usual. In need of change to meet the challenges of a new day, but "trapped in the tragic trap of tradition" as said by A. Louis Patterson, late pastor of the Mount Corinth Baptist Church in

Houston, Texas. Marriages and families are under attack, but the church is asleep. Men are conspicuously absent from the family and church, and the church is asleep. Children and youth are victims of a culture that is no longer family friendly and the church is comatose in activities that do not prepare them to live victorious in an unchristian world. An asleep church is scratching where nobody is itching. An asleep church is working where God is not at work. An asleep church is not focused on Christ's vision and strategy for His church, reaching the world with the Gospel of grace through making, marking, maturing and multiplying disciples, commencing at home. It is a church without aspiration for the future but trapped in yesterdays. This church has probably plateaued and has become complacent. When this sleeping church starts to decline it seeks to justify and spiritualize the decline, instead of encouraging new birth and growth. We must remember that where there is life there is growth, incarnationally and numerically, the kingdom of God is on the increase. There is mega ministry going on that might not result in attaining a mega church. The church that lives in the past has no future or, at least, no productive future. An asleep church is a passive church and will not effectively survive in the midst of evil aggressive trends. Healthy churches envision what can be in the context of God's purpose for His church.

Tradition is not bad in and of itself, except when, as someone once said, it is "success frozen." Non-traditional does not necessary mean new methodologies for ministry. I do not believe that the church is awake when it engages in twenty-first-century ministries, rather conversely, I think she must be awakened to engage in the first century ministry, that the last thing Jesus said ought not to be the least thing we do as church. *"Therefore, go into the world and make disciples"* (Matthew 28:19-20). Whatever the awake church does to reach the world with the Gospel of grace must be in the context of Christ's vision and strategy for His church. Why seek something new when we have not faithfully engaged in the old, evangelism through making, marking, maturing, and multiplying disciples?

Jonah was asleep on the job and going in the wrong direction. What direction is your church going in? When it comes to ministry, there is a way that appears to be right to some churches because it has the world's approval. In the days to come—and maybe it is already so—there will be state churches that are approved by the masses, for they will be more social than spiritual (Holy Spirit-driven spirituality). The sons of Issachar were not asleep for they *"understood the times, to know what Israel ought to do"* (1 Chronicles 12:32, NKJV). The awareness of the culture and times is necessary in ministering to the world the church is called to reach with the Gospel of grace. The church being asleep, not knowing what time it is—is sleepwalking and going in the wrong direction at the wrong time in history, which renders the church ineffective. However, we must not misinterpret the times and the condition of the church in these times. We must ask, what is happening and why is it happening? We must be introspective of the church's condition, but we dare not misinterpret the state of the church for from my vantage point, we do live in a post-Christian era of postmodernism, pluralism, naturalism, existentialism, and secularism. And we have been forewarned by the apostle Paul (2 Timothy 3:1-9) of these days and times. The falling away and the abandonment of the church by the young should alarm us, but not surprise us. Their leaving might be due to the fact that they were never of us (1 John 2:19). Perhaps, the church is guilty of churching our youth and not discipling them. Maybe we were asleep, thinking they were in, when they were in actuality outside the faith and the family of God. Maybe we were asleep, making them happy instead of holy. Now some may be prodigals, in time on their way back home, but in our critique of the church we must not only look at what is happening in the world and church, but why it is happening. So, I offer this list of what appears to be happening to keep us from slumbering in the storms of life:

The captain said to Jonah, *"How can you sleep at a time like this?"* And so, I pose this same question to the church. How can we sleep

- when 50% of the members are not certain of their salvation?
- when 60% to 70% of the members do not worship weekly?
- when 80% are not in Bible study and 50% of the leaders of the church refuse to attend Bible study?
- when 90% of church members have not been discipled?
- when over 85% are incapable of edifying the saints for the work of the ministry?
- when 80% of church members do very little serving and giving?
- when 70% give 1% or less of their total income to the work of the Lord?
- when humanistic and non-Christian religious worldviews are growing faster than the church's influence in the world?
- when prisons can't be built fast enough to house the number of criminals the system seeks to incarcerate?
- when our schools have been battlegrounds instead of learning centers?
- when millions of teenage girls are getting pregnant out of wedlock each year?
- when 60% of all church involved teenagers are sexually active?
- when every 78 seconds, a teenager in America attempts suicide?
- when millions of supposed members of the church are not really involved at all in the ministry of the church?
- when out of 22 million churchgoing evangelicals only 7% are prepared to share their Gospel story and only 2% actually do share their Gospel story?

- when Christians are not effectively penetrating the world nor their sphere of influence with the Gospel?

- when church pews are filled, but not Holy Spirit filled?

- when there are spiritually schizophrenic members whose belief and behavior are not congruent?

- when much of church growth is by transfer and not trans-generational and transformational?

- when there is a sin pandemic in the world and the Christian diaspora is not engaged in spreading the Gospel of grace in the world they were sent to evangelize?

The church must exist in the world with urgency for the coming of the Lord is nearer than when we first believed and became the church of Jesus Christ (John 4:35-38). This is harvest time. We must not sleep (see Romans 13:11-14; Ephesians 5:13-17). Having no concept of the imminent return of Christ can have a comatose effect on the Christians and church. In our slumber, we can become the reason for the storm. We can quell the storm if we awake from sleep and be the church of Jesus Christ. If we major in what Christ majored in, we can be effective in inclement weather. But we must arise from sleep, asking ourselves how can we sleep at a time like this?

The Church in Deception

> *"Then they said to him, 'Tell us, now! On whose account has this catastrophe struck us? What is your occupation, and where do you come from? What is your country, and from what people are you?' So he said to them, 'I am a Hebrew, and I fear the LORD God of heaven who made the sea and the dry land.'"*—Jonah 1:8-9, NASB

Jonah in his downward spiral of disobedience attempted to be somewhat invisible and concealed in the lower part of the ship in a storm of his own making. But the fingers were all pointing to him this runaway prophet attempting to run from the presence and purpose of the Lord. His being sleep in the storm uncovered him. How could he be asleep in a storm? This alerted the ungodly that something was awry. They sought to investigate this strange behavior in a storm. So, they interrogated Jonah. What is your business? Where do you come from? What country do you represent? Who do you belong to? Who are your people? Is the world today confused about the business of the church? Are we deceiving the world about who and whose we are? Do they know who we truly represent and that we are otherworldly? Are we acting contrary to the rest of the world? Jonah was in rebellion, but it was still obvious that there was something strange and different about him.

While the captain and crew discovered the runaway prophet, the Creator God never lost sight of him as he sought to go on strike, protesting his assignment, and take an unscheduled and unapproved vacation in Tarshish. And when it comes to the church living out Christ's purpose for His church, have we also taken a vacation? Have we sought to change our orders and go to Tarshish? Instead of making, marking, maturing, and multiplying disciples, have we gone to Tarshish to engage is social activism? Has the pressures of the world's opinion and the desire to be politically correct and socially relevant led the church of Jesus Christ to be other than the church of Jesus Christ, living in deception to her calling? Have we been forced by the world in another direction from Christ's purpose for His church in the world? Are we existing in the world as a fraudulent church claiming to be the church of Jesus Christ but being conformed to the world? Jonah was purposely hiding his identity. Is the church today confused concerning her identity and purpose?

This deception comes from misunderstanding the mission of Christ's church in the world. When we miss Christ's purpose, we will also miss the church's purpose for the church's business is to complete the unfinished work of Christ—reconciling the world back to God through the Word and ministry of reconciliation (2 Corinthians 5:18-21). When we see Christ's purpose on earth as social liberation, political confrontation, economic freedom and physical well-being, we will focus ministry on the wrong direction. Not that these concerns are not warranted of our attention, but they ought not be our primary focus. When we focus our attention on the miracles of Jesus and do not understand they were signs pointing beyond the miracles themselves to the authenticity of Jesus and the apostles, we are apt to lose our direction. It is plainly stated in Scripture that Jesus came to deliver us from the penalty and power of sin which is the root of all social problems in the world. The salvation of humanity was the main reason of the incarnation of God into the world in order to die in the place of sinners so that man could be reconciled back to God and live-in right relationship with God and man. The salvific purpose of the church will affect the total man, but it must start on the spiritual level and progress to the horizontal level of the social.

Jonah sailed with unbelievers and they did not know who he was, what he did, where he was from, nor who his people were. He lived in deception. In the midst of a storm, the church must be visible. The world must be clear about who we are and whose we are. The evidence must be conclusive that we are Jesus' witnesses and ambassadors. This is our business. We must tell the truth about Jesus in order that men may come to know Christ in salvation. It must be clear that we are not of this world, but we are otherworldly. We have been born from above. We are aliens and strangers in this world. It must be evident by our behavior that we are not from here. This will enable our proclamation of the Gospel of grace to be vividly heard. Jonah went with them towards Tarshish. The church must not go with the world, but be saints in the world, living differently from the world. We are not simply sinners saved by grace, but saints glorifying God. The church cannot afford to lose her identity as saints by blending into the world as sinners. The church cannot be broad in its proclamation and demonstration. We must not be intimidated by being the "few" nor overestimate the value of the "many" for Jesus said, *"Enter by the narrow gate. For the gate is wide and the way is easy that leads to destruction and those who enter by it are many. For the gate is narrow and the way is hard that leads to life, and those who find it are few"* (Matthew 7:13-14, ESV).

We cannot form an alliance with the religions of the world and be faithful to the mandate of Jesus. Jonah, after being confronted, declared who he really was and who he really represented: *"I am a Hebrew, and I fear the LORD God of heaven who made the sea and the dry land"* (Jonah 1:9, NASB). The church of Jesus Christ can have no affinity with other religions and certainly not any cults. Jonah announced the distinction of his faith and God.

The Church in Decline

> *"He said to them, 'Pick me up and hurl me into the sea. Then the sea will become calm for you, because I know that on account of me this great storm has come upon you.' . . . And the LORD designated a great fish to swallow Jonah, and Jonah was in the stomach of the fish for three days and three nights."*—Jonah 1:12, 17, NASB

A church can decline and die and still exist. It can function as an organization and at the same time does not function as an organism of Jesus Christ. Jonah was alive in the belly of the fish. He was alive in Sheol. He saw himself in a state of death in the fish's belly. He was not comfortable in that state, but some churches and members seem to be okay in decline and death. I have seen the churches and members happy with their condition just as long they have their tradition and titles. Declining churches are in the process of dying. There are no new spiritual births or physical births. There are no baptisms or baby dedications taking place in the membership. There is normally no functional children or youth ministries. Declining churches experience few visitors during their worship. These churches are mostly under the control of "old infants" who are stuck on maintenance goals and not driven by ministry goals. There is no zeal or excitement and anticipation in worship. Everything is tightly planned from the prelude to the postlude. In declining and dying churches, there is no talk of vision and strategy, or future aspirations. There is only vintage talk of the good old days. Like a church in deep sleep, a declining church is purposeless and powerless. It attempts to operate on its experience. It has learned to do ministry or church work so well that it doesn't need the Holy Spirit. It is all about regulations, rituals, religiosity and not relationship, either vertical or horizontal.

But sadly, there are other characteristics of churches that are in decline and dying. It is hard to detect these churches because they are much alive and exciting. They can be mega in size and ministry but heading in the wrong direction. They are living in deception, but self-deception for they have misconstrued the mission of Jesus in the world; therefore, they are declining in their purpose and dying spiritually in their focus. Decline must not be measured simply by numbers. If we use numerical decline as a church on its way to the grave, we are counting Jesus' ministry in that number for crowds left Him (John 6:66-71). Paul also announced that the church would experience a great falling away (2 Thessalonians 2:1-3). Please note this—in the visible church, decline and death will be experienced. Some because of Christ's doing, and others because the church is not doing the will of God (Revelation 2:5). There are some visible congregations that are out of Christ's will and purpose that might need to be removed and merged with another visible congregation.

Jonah went down and suffered decline in preparation for resurrection. Jonah's own sins took him down, but our sins took Jesus down and then

He was raised for our justification. Jonah was resurrected to complete God's purpose for his life. Jesus will also discipline His church to return to His purpose. Remember, that failure is not always final. Peter learned this truth through his denial of Jesus and also when walking with Jesus on water. Christ will rescue His church and His leaders (see John 21:15-17; Luke 22:32; Jonah 3:1).

Declining churches are not merely declining in numbers, but in fulfilling the biblical purpose for the church. Some churches appear to be growing when indeed that might be simply swelling. The numbers are there, but the incarnational growth is not evident. Churches do not have to be mega to be effective. The mega church is really not the normal situation. Probably the better definition or description of a declining church is that it is non-productive. Another way to describe a church in decline is that it is an unhealthy church. According to Rick Warren, a church's health is measured by its sending capacity not its seating capacity.[38] A growing church is not necessarily a megachurch, but a healthy church that is missional in purpose. A healthy church can be a community of believers committed to developing disciples and sending them into the world to make, mark, mature, and multiply disciples where they live, work, learn and play. A declining church is a church that is not on a mission for the sake of Jesus Christ.

We have identified the "Jonah Baptist Church of Tarshish," which is a sad state of affairs. For it is the church in defiance, in deep sleep, in deception and in decline. But thanks be to God, He is the God of resurrection and deliverance. The "Jonah Baptist Church of Tarshish" can become the "Jonah Baptist Church of Nineveh," doing the will of God.

The Church Delivered

> *"The word of the LORD came to Jonah the second time, saying, 'Arise, go to Nineveh, the great city, and proclaim to it the proclamation which I am going to tell you.' So Jonah got up and went*

to Nineveh according to the word of the LORD. Now Nineveh was an exceedingly large city, a three days' walk. Then Jonah began to go through the city one day's walk; and he cried out and said, 'Forty more days, and Nineveh will be overthrown.'"
—Jonah 3:1-4, NASB

Years ago, I asked Dr. Elliot Mason, a former pastor of the Trinity Baptist Church in Los Angeles, California, who is now in the presence the Lord, did he see spiritual renewal in the church's future? He exclaimed, "Yes, but after judgment." He spoke of judgment as discipline. In Hebrews, we are told, *"For the Lord disciplines the one he loves and chastises every son whom he receives. It is for discipline that you have to endure. God is treating you as sons. For what son is there whom his father does not discipline? If you are left without discipline, in which all have participated, then you are illegitimate children and not sons"* (Hebrews 12:6-8, ESV). Jonah had to experience the depth of the consequences of disobedience. God the Father ordered and planned Jonah's discipline. The Lord prepared a large fish to imprison him. He experienced death without dying. He experienced hell without actually going there. He experienced the absence of God. He wanted to flee from the presence of God, but he had no idea how horrible it would be away from God. As Abraham found out, it is better to be in a famine with God than to be in the midst of a feast without God. The faraway country taught the Prodigal Son that it is better to stay in fellowship with the father. It took the experience of the faraway country for the Prodigal to come to himself.

It took being in a type of hell for Jonah to cry out to God in prayer. He had to be hemmed in, helpless, and expelled from the presence of the Lord before his prayer lined up according to God's will. Prayer caused him to look in the right direction as he again looked towards the holy temple. He had stopped looking in God's direction and thus lost his direction. When he stopped looking in God's direction, he ended up engulfed by the water of life and wrapped in the weeds of the world. But in his hell, he remembered the Lord. While he was fainting away, he remembered the Lord and prayed and had confidence that the Lord heard him. His God was not like idol gods who have ears but cannot hear, eyes but cannot see, legs but cannot come to his rescue, and arms but cannot deliver. In the belly of the fish, Jonah worshipped and thanked God. Before his prayer was answered, he worshipped and thanked the Lord. He did not wait until he got back to Jerusalem, he worshipped and thanked God in the belly of the fish. Prayer changed Jonah's attitude towards God. He allowed his attitude towards the Ninevites to affect his attitude towards God. But now he looks again towards the holy temple.

When the church is in decline, only God can deliver. Jonah said, "*Salvation is from the LORD*" (Jonah 2:9, NASB). He realized that he was in need of deliverance. In salvation and in sanctification, one cannot be delivered until he or she knows that they are in need of salvation and deliverance. Also, a church in decline must recognize it is declining before deliverance can come. It is a dangerous thing to succeed without repentance. The devil has a way of helping Christians and churches to succeed without repentance. It is pseudo success. For no success is genuine that does not bring glory to God through obedience. The psalmist said, "*God takes no delight in sacrifices of offering, but in doing God's will*" (Psalm 40:6, 8, NASB—paraphrased).

After Jonah recognized his need of God's deliverance, then God intervened and reversed the decline. "*Then the LORD commanded the fish, and it vomited Jonah up onto the dry land*" (Jonah 2:10, NASB). Recorded in 2 Chronicles is an antidote for a declining church or people. Although, this passage is not to us, there are principles in the passage for us. To a certain extent, we can apply the passage to the church. We cannot use this passage in a literal sense as it refers to Israel, for we have not been promised material blessings like them. However, the church has been promised spiritual blessings. "*Blessed be the God and Father of our Lord Jesus Christ, who has blessed us with every spiritual blessing in the heavenly places in*

Christ" (Ephesians 1:3, NASB). Therefore, we approach 2 Chronicles 7:14 with a sense of limited application for the church. If the declining and dying church is to be diverted, experiencing deliverance, these five things need to happen. As people of prayer,

1) we must understand that we are God's people.

2) we must humble ourselves and get rid of pride.

3) we must pray as an act of dependence on God.

4) we must seek the face and favor of God by desiring to please Him.

5) we must turn and go in the right direction, a radical shift in God's direction for the church.

This is repentance. Resurrection and deliverance come after there are effectual prayers of the righteous (James 5:16).

A Glorious Church

"*Do you hear them coming, brother? Thronging up the steeps of light, clad in glorious shining garments, blood-washed garments pure and white. Do you hear the stirring anthems, filling all the earth and sky? 'Tis a grand, victorious army; lift its banner up on high! Never fear the clouds of sorrow, never fear the storms of sin; we shall triumph on the morrow—even now our joys begin. Wave the banner, shout His praises, for our victory is nigh! Following our conquering Savior, we shall reign with Him on high!*

'Tis a glorious church without spot or wrinkle, washed in the blood of the Lamb; 'Tis a glorious church without spot or wrinkle, washed in the blood of the Lamb."[39]

Notes

1. Lloyd Ogilvie, *The Autobiography of God*, Baker Publishing Group, 2013.

2. C. Norman Kraus, *The Authentic Witness*, Wm. B. Eerdmans Publishing Co. Grand Rapids, Michigan, 1979, p. 23.

3. Ibid., p. 71.

4. Ibid., p. 97.

5. Ibid., p. 97.

6. Jürgen Moltmann, *The Church in the Power of the Spirit*, Harper & Row, Publishers, New York, 1977, p. 72.

7. Ibid., p. 72.

8. Tony Evans, *God's Glorious Church*, Moody Publishers, Chicago, 2003, p. 37.

9. John R. W. Stott, *The Message of Ephesians*, Leicester, England: Inter-Varsity Press, 1979, p. 146.

10. John F. MacArthur, *The MacArthur New Testament Commentary*, Ephesians, Chicago: Moody Press, 1986, p. 120.

11. Ibid., p. 122.

12. John R. W. Stott, *The Message of Ephesians Commentary*, Leicester, England: Inter-Varsity Press, 1979, p. 149.

13. *The Nicene Creed* (AD 325) in the City of Nicene.

14. John R. W. Stott, *The Message of Ephesians*, Leicester, England: Inter-Varsity Press, 1979, p. 155-156.

15 John F. MacArthur, *The MacArthur New Testament Commentary on First Corinthians,* Chicago, Moody Press; 1984. p. 283.

16 Ibid., p. 283.

17 John F. MacArthur, *Spiritual Gifts,* Chicago: Moody Press, 1983, p. 30.

18 Ibid., pp. 64-65.

19 John F. MacArthur, *The MacArthur New Testament Commentary,* Ephesians, Chicago: Moody Press, 1986, p. 157.

20 D. M. Lloyd Jones, *God's Ultimate Purpose,* Vol. 1, Grand Rapids: Baker Book House, 1979, p. 431.

21 D. M. Lloyd Jones, *Christian Unity: Ephesians,* Grand Rapids: Baker Book House, 1981, p. 272.

22 Francis Chan, *Forgotten God,* David C. Cook Publisher, Colorado Springs, 2009, p. 15.

23 Ray C. Stedman, *Body Life, A division of G/L Publications,* Glendale, California, 1952, p. 15.

24 C. Norman Kraus, *The Authentic Witness,* WM. B. Eerdmans Publishing Co. Grand Rapids, Michigan, 1979, p. 31.

25 Fred Campbell, *Discipleship according to Jesus,* Sunday School Publishing Board, Nashville Tennessee, 2019.

26 R. H. Cornelius, "Oh, I Want to See Him," 1916.

27 Fred Fisher, *The Sermon on the Mount:* Broadman Press, Nashville, Tennessee, 1976, p. 38.

28 Robert Guelich, *The Sermon on the Mount:* Word Publishing, Dallas Texas, 1982, p. 105.

29 Edward Mote, "The Solid Rock," 1863.

30 John Thompson and Randy Scruggs, "Sanctuary," Whole Armor Publishing, New York, NY, 1982.

31 John MacArthur, *The MacArthur New Testament Commentary (Matthew)* Moody Bible Publisher, Chicago, 1989, p. 271.

32 Mike Mason, *The Mystery of Marriage,* Multnomah Press, Portland Oregon, 1985, p. 137.

33 John MacArthur, *The MacArthur New Testament Commentary, (1 Timothy)* Moody Press, Chicago, Ill. 1995, p. 108

34 Sandy F. Ray, *Journeying through a Jungle,* Broadman Press, Nashville, Tennessee, 1979, p. 33.

35 Warren W. Wiersbe, *The Bible Exposition Commentary,* Chariot Victor Publishing, Colorado Springs, Colorado, 1989, p. 362.

36 Ibid., p. 362.

37 Dr. S. M. Lockridge, *The Challenge of the Church,* Zondervan Publishing House, Grand Rapids, 1969, p. 9.

38 Rick Warren, *The Purpose Driven Church,* Zondervan Publishing House, Grand Rapids, 1995, p. 32.

39 Ralph E. Hudson, "A Glorious Church," Hymn.

References

Allison, G. R. and A. J. Köstenberger. *The Holy Spirit*. Nashville, TN: B & H Publishing Group, 2020.

Azurdia, A. G. III. *Spirit Empowered Mission*. Scotland: Christian Focus Publications, 2016.

Barna, G., and D. Kinnaman. *Churchless*. Tyndale House Publishers, Inc., 2014.

Berkhof, H. *The Doctrine of the Holy Spirit*. Atlanta, GA: John Knox Press, 1946.

Bloesch, D. G. *Essentials of Evangelical Theology*, vol. 1. San Francisco, CA: Harper & Row Publishers, 1978.

Bruner, F. D. *A Theology of the Holy Spirit*. Grand Rapids, MI: William B. Eerdmans Publisher, 1970.

Evans, T. *God's Glorious Church*. Chicago, IL: Moody Press, 2003.

_____. *Theology You Can Count On*. Chicago, IL: Moody Publishers, 2008.

Getz, G. A. *Elders and Leaders*. Chicago, IL: Moody Publishers, 2003.

Harris, M. M. *The Church that Christ Builds*. 2020.

Hobbs, H. H. *Fundamentals of Our Faith*. Nashville, TN: Broadman Press, 1960.

Kraus, C. N. *The Authentic Witness*. Grand Rapids, MI: William B. Eerdmans Publishing Company, 1979.

MacArthur, J. *Christ's Call to Reform the Church*. Chicago, IL: Moody Publishers, 2018.

_____. *Spiritual Gifts (1 Corinthians)*. Chicago, IL: Moody Press, 1983.

Rainer, T. S. and S. Rainer III. *Essential Church?* Nashville, TN: B & H Publishing Group, 2008.

Rogers, A. *What Every Christian Ought to Know*. Nashville, TN: B & H Publishing Group, 2005.

Smith, R. Jr. *Doctrine that Dances*. Nashville, TN: B & H Academic, 2008.

Strong, A. H. *Systematic Theology*. Philadelphia, PA: Judson Press, 1907.

Swindoll, C. R. *The Bride*. Grand Rapids, MI: Zondervan Publishing House, 1994.

Thiessen, H. C. *Lectures in Systematic Theology*. Grand Rapids, MI: William B. Eerdmans Publishing Company, 1949.

Warren, R. *The Purpose Driven Church*. Grand Rapids, MI: Zondervan Publishing House, 1995.

About the Author

Pastor Fred Campbell

Pastor Fred Campbell has served as Mt. Zion Baptist Church's pastor for more than forty years, being one of the longest-tenured pastors in the San Francisco Bay Area. His innovative and proven leadership has left an indelible mark, leading people towards spiritual maturity. Over the span of his Gospel ministry, he has been a champion for discipleship, faith at home, education, empowering men, and more. Members enjoy his biblically sound preaching and teaching, humor, and personable demeanor. He is currently leading Mt. Zion in pursuing the win, where each member grows in relationship with Jesus and into maturity in the body of Christ.

Pastor Campbell is one of our nation's trailblazing leaders, serving in various capacities throughout his ministry. He has served in the California State Baptist Convention, Inc., in various leadership positions, including financial secretary, Christian education director, and Congress of Christian Education president. In 2002, under the mantra of "Building Healthy Churches," he became president of the California State Baptist Convention, guiding it in becoming a viable resource to local churches. Borne out of his service to our state convention, Pastor Campbell is also a leader in the National Baptist Convention, USA, Inc. He served under the Shaw Administration as historian, at-large board member under the Scruggs Administration, and chairman of the board under the Young Administration.

Pastor Campbell has a deep passion for pastors, ministers, and their wives and provides wise counsel and support to pastors throughout the nation. In 2001 he and his wife, Joyce, founded Shepherd's Tent Ministries, a ministry that supports pastors, ministers, and their wives. This ministry now hosts the Word Conference, one of the premier conferences on the West Coast promoting biblical education and literacy.

He is a graduate of California Baptist University in Riverside, California, and Golden Gate Baptist Theological Seminary in Mill Valley, California.

Pastor Campbell was married to Joyce Elane Campbell for more than forty-nine years before her passing in 2011. He has six children and five grandchildren.

www.ingramcontent.com/pod-product-compliance
Lightning Source LLC
Chambersburg PA
CBHW072010110526
44592CB00012B/1259